Brassicas

LAURA B. RUSSELL

Photography by Sang An

Brassicas

Cooking the World's
Healthiest Vegetables:
Kale, Cauliflower, Broccoli,
Brussels Sprouts and More

TEN SPEED PRESS
Berkeley

Foreword BY REBECCA KATZ

When Hippocrates said "Let food be thy medicine, and medicine be thy food," there's little doubt in my mind that he was referring to foods drawn from the brassica family. Ounce for ounce, brassicas contain more healing properties than any other branch of food. We're not just talking your basic building blocks of vitamins and minerals—though brassicas are full of these—but foods also rich in phytochemicals that act as anticarcinogenics (anticancer), anti-inflammatories, and promote liver detoxification.

Even though these foods have been around for eons, it's only in the last few years that science is unraveling all the goodness that brassicas have to offer. In fact, if you're reading about brassicas here for the first time, consider yourself ahead of the curve; I recently spoke to an audience of 300 nurses, and when I asked for a show of hands of those who knew what brassicas were, maybe a dozen hands went up.

Why is there so little public awareness of these superfoods? Maybe brassicas are in need of a good PR campaign, à la the dancing California Raisins; all I know is there's plenty of raw material to work with. There are more than a dozen brassicas you've probably heard of, including veggies such as broccoli, cauliflower, cabbage, and Brussels sprouts. Each is a nutritional powerhouse. Broccoli warehouses vitamin K, essential in promoting bone health and reducing the impact of osteoporosis. Cauliflower is loaded, as are many brassicas, with glucosinolates that keep the immune system from overreacting: Such overreaction may be a major player in wrecking health, as it can lead to the kind of chronic inflammation now being linked to cardiovascular disease and certain cancers. In fact, studies show glucosinolates in brassicas may play a role in knocking down a host of cancers, including those that occur in the lungs and alimentary canal (a fancy name that means our entire 20-foot-long digestive tract). Cabbage is rich in a specific phytochemical, indole-3-carbinol, which promotes the liver's removal of estrogen from the body, a benefit to women concerned with hormone-related breast cancer. Brussels sprouts have chemicals believed to play a role in keeping the body's DNA intact and functioning properly.

In a sense, brassicas are like tiny mechanics, constantly doing tune-ups throughout the body. We certainly need the help; cellular metabolism is amazing but messy, constantly spewing forth toxic by-products that need to be flushed from the system.

A brassica such as kale is a one-man maintenance shop; its high fiber binds with cholesterol to sweep unnecessary fat out of the body, and it's been shown to inhibit inflammation associated with arthritis.

I could go on and on, citing study after study. It doesn't matter which brassica you're looking at—collard greens, horseradish, arugula, even wasabi—the health benefits are enormous. Which begs the question: if brassicas are so good for you, why do we let these power hitters so often ride the pine instead of making their way to the plate?

The simple answer is that, at first glance, brassicas are often pretty darn unwieldy. The aforementioned kale is a big mound of leaves, cabbage looks like a bowling ball, and purple cauliflower resembles something you'd see in a science fiction movie or perhaps a Zombie flick. *Braiiiiiiiinnnnnssssssss!!!!*

It takes a certain amount of culinary courage to go one on one with a brassica for the first time. You can feel like you need a machete, but as Laura Russell so wonderfully explains, a sharp large knife and a good cutting board can whittle any brassica down to size quickly and efficiently. Aside from their sheer bulk, brassicas have a reputation for being bitter tasting, notably for a sizable percentage of the population who are so-called "supertasters," aka, folks born with extremely sensitive taste buds. Let's face it, most of us encountered brassicas when we were young, and if the cook didn't know how to counter the pungency we ended up looking at the brassica with disdain, a nasty "pill" of culinary medicine to be swallowed.

That's why it is such a delight to see Russell elevate the brassicas' taste to a place commensurate with their superstar nutritional prowess. Each recipe in this book delivers on that promise, and as a cook I can appreciate the time and effort that Laura has put into these creative recipes. I often think of brassicas as the emeralds of the food world, so valuable are they to maintaining and promoting health. In this book, Laura Russell allows all of us to partake of their wealth, with dishes that will entice us to go for our greens, again and again.

For this, I can only give thanks. Enjoy!

Rebecca Katz, MS
author of *The Longevity Kitchen* and *Cancer Fighting Kitchen*

Introduction

There has never been a more important time to make the connection between food and health. With the sharp rise in obesity, food allergies and sensitivities, and a growing distrust of processed foods, the Standard American Diet (SAD) is nearing an inflection point. Thankfully, a national dialogue has been stirred that puts the responsibility for what we eat firmly on our own shoulders. As that discussion matures, people will come to realize that their food choices are not only about immediate sustenance, but also the best sources of preventative medicine for long-term well-being.

Despite this promising dialogue, there is a growing disconnect between the overwhelming nutritional choices available to us and our ability to end up with a healthful meal. We surf through this information explosion, and deal with frequently contradictory dietary directives, yet fewer of us are equipped with the time or the skill set to make our real-life kitchens work. Consequently, when faced with the straightforward instruction to "eat more vegetables," it's hard to know where to begin.

Why not start with the wildly diverse group of vegetables known as brassicas? Also called crucifers, they belong to the big Brassicaceae family, sometimes known more simply as the mustard family or cabbage family. Brassicas are chock-full of vitamins, minerals, and sulfur-rich phytonutrients that aid in cancer prevention (see page vii). For many people, though, these nutritional powerhouses suffer from an image problem. Who hasn't thought of Grandma's stinky boiled cabbage or a mound of watery overcooked cauliflower? In contrast, the brassicas I imagine include a captivating range of vegetables: leafy greens, verdant stems, flowering heads, and pungent roots. I think of the inherent sweetness that can be coaxed from properly roasted Brussels sprouts, or the bright, peppery punch of a simple watercress and arugula salad. And what about the oft-forgotten mustard greens, whose pungency can be played as an attribute when paired with the sweetness of jammy caramelized onions? Even a sneeze-inducing horseradish sauce never fails to capture my attention. These are my kinds of brassicas, and I want you in on the fun.

In a perfect world, we would all enjoy Saturday morning farmers' market visits to pick up glistening fresh produce for the week. Such markets overflow with beautiful brassicas in shapes, colors, and varieties that never appear in supermarkets. If you have one in your area, be sure to check it out and support your local farmers. But farmers' markets are not where most people shop. Throughout this book, I have assumed that you shop for vegetables at a supermarket. Commonplace brassicas—broccoli, cauliflower, cabbage, kale, Brussels sprouts—account for more than half of the recipes in these pages, but some of my other favorites, like collard greens, kohlrabi, and broccoli rabe, are also deserving of your attention. A few of the harder-to-find vegetables—Chinese broccoli, mizuna, or tatsoi—may require a trip to an Asian market, but I always offer readily available substitutes in these recipes.

As we start cooking together, I will dispel the notion that brassicas must endure death-by-boiling—possibly the worst way to prepare them—or burial under a thick blanket of cheese. Instead, I'll guide you toward cooking methods that play to each vegetable's strengths, favoring those that celebrate the intrinsic flavors instead of masking them. Cooking should be fun, not intimidating, so I have created eighty recipes that will enable you to incorporate vegetables throughout your day—a frittata or Spanish tortilla for breakfast, soups and salads, side dishes, snacks, and even a smoothie! Some recipes demonstrate the most straightforward way to cook a vegetable, such as simply sautéed kale, roasted rutabagas, or stir-fried bok choy. Other recipes, like a Moroccan-inspired braise of turnips and chickpeas, take you to the next level without being overly complicated. For anyone with food sensitivities, the Special Diets Table on page 158–159 labels each recipe for the most common allergens and food intolerances as well as whether it is vegan, vegetarian, or neither. (I did not take the easy way out by throwing bacon on everything, but pork does make an appearance in a handful of the recipes, as does fish sauce.) All of the recipes are gluten-free.

Once we explore the brassica family together, I hope you will grow increasingly interested in pushing past those plain boiled vegetables in favor of some lighthearted kitchen experimentation. If you do, I guarantee you will discover many new favorites along the way.

Brassica Basics

When I hear the word *brassica*, my mind immediately begins to race with possibilities. Should I caramelize Brussels sprouts and dust them with pecorino cheese? Or, perhaps I'll quickly toss together a kale salad with a zesty lemon vinaigrette? These vegetables never fail to excite me, yet nearly every time I utter the word *brassica*, I am met with blank stares and confused looks by everyone except chefs and gardeners. So before we begin cooking brassicas together, I need to introduce my favorite vegetable clan.

As I noted in the Introduction, brassicas belong to the family of plants known as Brassicaceae. In the past, the same family was called Cruciferae, named for the four-petal cross formed by the flowers of its members. Because both botanical names are still used, brassicas are also often called crucifers or cruciferous vegetables. The family includes more than three hundred genera, one of which is also called *Brassica* and is home to such big-name stars as cabbage, cauliflower, Brussels sprouts, and broccoli. Nearly every part of a plant within this sprawling botanical clan is used for food: roots (radishes), stems (kohlrabi), leaves (kale), flowers (broccoli florets), stalks (bok choy), buds (Brussels sprouts), sprouts, and seeds (mustard).

Sadly, brassicas as a whole have an unwarranted reputation for having strong flavors and smells. Yes, some of them can overwhelm any other vegetable in the kitchen. But their flavors are far more nuanced than those extreme descriptions imply, ranging from sweet and grassy all the way up to hot and spicy.

Flavor Profiles

The spectrum of flavors represented by the brassicas makes them one of the most compelling vegetable groups to cook. Here, I have divided them among four broad categories—mild, stronger, peppery, and pungent—that offer a quick glance into their general flavor intensity. (Each chapter introduction includes a more detailed flavor description.) Keep in mind that you may taste differences due to seasonality, climate, or regional variation. For example, radishes are typically "hotter" in the summer than in the fall, and kale sown in the fall in cooler areas yields a sweeter, nuttier flavor than kale from hot climates. Some brassicas have characteristics that fall into more than one flavor category—bok choy stalks, for example, are sweet and juicy, while the leaves are more full flavored—and those I have tucked into the group that suits them best overall.

MILD

These vegetables can taste sweet, juicy, nutty, or grassy. Some bites finish with a mild, pleasant hint of pepper or bitterness, but nothing that overwhelms.

STRONGER

Although these vegetables boast more pronounced flavors than the mild group, they can still be described as earthy, sweet, grassy, minerally, and pleasantly bitter. But if you mistakenly overcook them, especially cabbage, broccoli, and Brussels sprouts, those appealing characteristics will be immediately replaced by a completely different and rather unpleasant (sulfurous) set of traits.

PEPPERY

Count on this group to reveal a distinctive peppery burst of flavor. Spring turnips and daikon radishes come on quite gently—crisp and mild with a peppery finish; the others make their case more assertively. Leafy arugula and cress, albeit innocent looking from afar, often taste downright spicy, though their heat is irresistible.

PUNGENT

Mustard greens can be hard to classify because so many varieties exist, some mild enough for salads and others much too sharply flavored. When it comes to horseradish, wasabi, or powdered mustard, think "sinus clearing." The most satisfying bites of these brassicas end with a sneeze.

MILD
Bok choy
Cauliflower
Chinese broccoli (*gai lan*)
Kohlrabi
Mizuna
Napa cabbage
Rutabaga
Tatsoi

STRONGER
Broccoli
Broccolini
Broccoli rabe
Brussels sprouts
Cabbage
Collard greens
Kale
Romanesco cauliflower

PEPPERY
Arugula
Upland cress
Radishes
Turnips
Watercress

PUNGENT
Horseradish
Mustard greens, seeds and prepared mustard
Wasabi

Taming the Beast: Turning Bold Flavors into Tasty Dishes

The first rule when cooking boldly flavored vegetables is never to equate the words *strong* or *bitter* with unpleasant. When properly handled, these flavors will add excitement to your plate rather than overwhelm their neighbors. You just need a plan. Here are my three go-to strategies: find a counterpoint to balance the flavors, match bold with bold, or add heat.

1. BALANCE

Think about super-peppery arugula leaves or sharp mustard greens that taste too intense to eat on their own. What can you add to make them more delicious? (Hint: There's a reason why the ubiquitous arugula salad with goat cheese, figs, and balsamic vinaigrette tastes so good.) Here are some options:

- Add something starchy or bland to soften the flavors. Try beans, potatoes, polenta, rice, or pasta.

- Add dairy. The creaminess (and fat content) of butter, yogurt, cheese, sour cream, or milk will smooth out aggressive flavors.

- Add a hint of sweetness. Honey, agave nectar, caramelized onions, dried or fresh fruit, coconut, tomatoes, or balsamic vinegar will lighten the intensity. For example, stirring caramelized onions into wilted mustard greens disarms their pungency completely.

- Add fat to marry the flavors. Try olive oil, coconut oil, nut oils, butter or other dairy products, coconut milk, avocado, nuts, or egg.

2. BOLD ON BOLD

Sometimes the best way to complement assertive flavors is to stand right up to them. Have you ever wondered why chefs sauté broccoli rabe with anchovies and red pepper flakes? That's bold on bold. I like to prepare these intensely flavorful side dishes and pair them with simple mains, like grilled chicken, steak, or burgers. Here are some ideas:

- Add spiciness. Brassicas pair particularly well with red pepper flakes, cayenne pepper, and fresh chiles. Or, use the pungent brassicas—mustard, horseradish, or wasabi—to season the others.

- Add salt. Anchovies, capers, olives, bacon, pancetta, soy sauce, fish sauce, and hard grating cheeses like Parmesan or pecorino make marvelous companions to loud flavors.

3. HEAT

Heat mellows harsh edges. Even simple wilting will do. That's why young, tender mustard greens taste great tossed with a warm bacon dressing, or the bite of arugula is tempered atop a hot cheesy pizza. And many brassicas, such as broccoli rabe, broccoli, and cauliflower, simply taste better cooked than raw. Just be sure not to overcook brassicas, or you may *activate* stronger flavors in the milder-tasting ones.

Anchovies
Beans, dried or shelled
Bell peppers, red
Butter
Capers
Cheeses, hard or salty (Parmesan, pecorino, feta)
Chiles
Cumin
Dill
Eggs
Fish sauce
Garlic
Ginger
Lemon
Mint
Mushrooms
Mustard (prepared, powdered, or seeds)
Nuts (especially almonds, pistachios, walnuts)
Olive oil
Olives
Onions
Parsley
Pasta
Polenta
Pork, cured (bacon, pancetta, prosciutto)
Potatoes
Rice
Sesame oil
Soy sauce
Yogurt

Universal Pairings: Brassicas' Best Friends

You need only three things to make nearly any brassica taste delicious: olive oil, garlic, and salt. With these in hand you can turn out a quick sauté, a pan full of roasted vegetables, or (add lemon juice) a salad. Because the brassicas are all members of the same botanical family, it makes sense that they share an affinity for certain pairings. The ingredients to the left mate well with most of the family members.

Selection, Storage, and Prep Tips

There is very little standardization in vegetable "packaging." For example, you can walk up to the meat counter and order a pound of ground beef, but in the vegetable department, a "bunch" of kale may weigh anywhere from 6 to 14 ounces, or a "head" of broccoli may be a single 8-ounce crown or a few stalks bundled together in plastic. Because of this, if you don't already own a kitchen scale, I highly recommend that you purchase one to ensure accurate measurements. I use mine every day. In case you don't have a scale, however, I have included more than one unit of measurement for brassicas in recipes where the amount can vary because of how they are packaged. For example, I might call for 1 large bunch kale (12 to 14 ounces), or if I call for a head of broccoli, I will include the amount of florets in cups, as well. You might also take the time to weigh your vegetables where you shop. A supermarket produce department always has a scale or two, and smaller stores and sometimes farmers' markets often have scales, too.

My other issue with the absence of standardization is waste. If I call for 1 pound Brussels sprouts in a recipe and your store sells them in 12-ounce bags, I don't want you to purchase two bags if you won't use them. It is better to adjust the seasonings to adapt to the quantity you have.

I have provided advice on selection and storage of specific vegetables in each chapter introduction, but here are some general tips. Always choose brassicas that looks fresh and vibrant, avoiding any that are wilting, yellowing, or showing any other signs of aging. Time and excess water are the enemies of good storage. When you unload your groceries, remove any rubber bands or twist ties from bunched greens. If the greens are wet, that binding will promote rot in the center of the bunch. For a similar reason, remove tight plastic packaging from cauliflower or broccoli, as it traps moisture directly against the vegetable. If the vegetable has both edible leaves and stems or roots (radishes, kohlrabies, turnips), cut the leaves from the rest of the vegetable and store them separately. Most vegetables keep well in a loosely sealed plastic bag with a paper towel tucked inside to wick away extra moisture.

A note on paper and plastic: I find that storing vegetables with a paper towel extends their life and thus eliminates waste. Assuming the towels are still in good shape, I reuse them, moving them from one bag to a new one. If you don't like this idea, pick up some cotton tea towels and use them for wicking excess moisture. I also reuse my plastic bags over and over until they are spent. Or, you can store your vegetables in fine-mesh polyester bags or even reusable containers. Don't seal the lid of the container, however, or you will trap moisture that will hasten spoilage.

Washing Greens

Greens can be surprisingly dirty and usually need more than just a quick rinse. You can wash the leaves whole or cut them first, as you like. (I usually shred kale, collard greens, and even cabbage leaves before I wash them.) Put a large bowl in the sink and fill it with cool water. Add the greens and swish them around with your hands. Lift the greens out of the water and put them in a colander in the sink or in a salad spinner. (Don't dump out the water with the greens or the dirt will go right back onto them.) Pour out the water and dirt, rinse the bowl, and repeat until when you pour out the rinsing water, no dirt is visible.

If you are making a salad, dry the washed greens well to avoid diluting the dressing. I also dry greens that I'll be cooking, but it's less important to dry them completely, as a bit of water clinging to the leaves should not hurt the dish. If you want to salvage greens that look a little wilted but are still fresh enough to eat, soak them in a bowl of ice water for a few minutes to perk them up. I often do this with radish greens.

To wash root brassicas—radishes, turnips, rutabagas, horseradish—and kohlrabi, scrub them gently under running water. Cut broccoli, cauliflower, bok choy, or Brussels sprouts as directed in the recipe and rinse them in a colander under running water.

V Cut

Some greens, kale and collards specifically and sometimes mustard, turnip, and kohlrabi greens, have a thick, fibrous center rib that is unpleasant to chew. I always remove this rib, which is located smack dab in the center of the leaf, as well as the stems of all but the tiniest, most delicate leaves. In some cases, you can fold the leaf in half lengthwise and simply "unzip" the stem and rib with your fingers. If that method removes too much of the actual leaf, use the V-cut method: Put a leaf on a cutting board and fold it in half lengthwise, with the tough stem facing out. Cut alongside the rib and stem to remove them from the leaf and then discard them. When you open the leaf flat, it will have an open V shape at its center. Proceed with washing and cutting the greens as directed.

This technique may sound time-consuming, but you will enjoy eating these greens more without the chewy ribs. I actually relish the repetitive nature of the task, but if I'm too busy, I pawn the job off on my ten-year-old, who loves acting as my sous chef. It's a great way to teach knife skills, and she gets it done quickly with just a paring knife.

Techniques That Make Brassicas Shine

My theory on why so many people think they don't like brassicas revolves around how the vegetables are prepared. When I ask the naysayers how they cook broccoli, cauliflower, and Brussels sprouts, they nearly always reply that they boil them. That's not to say that there is no place for simply boiled and buttered vegetables on your table—it is certainly quick and easy. But boiling brassicas breaks down their cell walls (releasing sulfur compounds) faster and more aggressively than any other cooking method, which can produce unpleasant odors and also lead to overcooking. Plus, because boiled vegetables are cooked in a large quantity of water, they retain excess liquid after you drain them. So, if you do not pat them quite dry, they can have a watery taste. Boiled vegetables can be also be pretty boring, unless you take time to dress them up. Since many other techniques better highlight the qualities that make brassicas delicious, I invite you to give them a try.

Roasting: If you want quick and easy, this technique is for you. Cut vegetables into small pieces, toss them with olive oil and salt directly on a rimmed baking sheet, and slip them into a hot oven. Serve the vegetables straight from the pan to minimize dirty dishes. The key here is to use a baking sheet large enough to accommodate the vegetables in a single layer (try an 18 by 13-inch pan, known as a half sheet pan), so they have a chance to caramelize. If you do not have a large baking sheet, use two smaller ones. Just be sure they are rimmed or you'll be picking up little pieces of cauliflower off the floor.

Sautéing: This is my go-to method for cooking leafy greens like kale and collards. Once again, the key here is to use a pan that is large enough to hold the vegetables comfortably. You will likely need a frying pan or sauté pan that is *at least* 12 inches wide. A smaller pan will not be able to handle a large quantity of bulky greens before they are wilted or accommodate chunkier vegetables like cauliflower or Brussels sprouts in a single layer. If your goal is to caramelize the vegetables, they need to come in contact with the hot surface of the pan rather than be piled high above it.

Stir-frying: Brassicas make fabulous additions to stir-fries, either alone or in combination with one another. Cut them into small pieces suitable for quick, high-heat cooking. Harder vegetables, like broccoli or cauliflower, can be blanched (boiled) for a minute or two to get the cooking started (be sure to dry them well afterward), or just you can cut them into very small pieces. Add tender leafy brassicas, like bok choy leaves, tatsoi, or watercress, toward the end of cooking.

Grilling: Not every brassica takes well to grilling, but broccoli, halved heads of baby bok choy, cauliflower planks, cabbage wedges, and kohlrabi slices all fare well with a trip to the flames. Toss with olive oil and salt and grill over a medium to medium-hot fire until done. (If grilling over direct heat doesn't soften the vegetables as much as you like, try cooking them over indirect heat and covering the grill for a few minutes.) If you plan to grill vegetables frequently, pick up a grill screen to set over the grate so the vegetables won't slip between the bars.

Moist-heat cooking: Soups, stews, and braises, where the liquid is a flavorful component of the dish, are excellent vehicles for brassicas. Lightly steamed vegetables are ideal when you are looking for something truly simple. Set up a collapsible steamer basket in a large pot over (not touching) an inch or two of boiling water and steam the vegetables for just a few minutes. Blanching is useful if you want to jump-start the cooking of firm-textured vegetables, tone down the flavor of a particularly powerful bunch of broccoli rabe, or reduce a giant pile of greens to a manageable quantity. Bring a big pot of water to a boil and cook the vegetables quickly, just for a minute or two, while keeping the water at a boil. Drain them well or, in the case of leafy greens, you may need to wring them out if they are headed for the sauté pan.

Wilting: You may think of greens like watercress and arugula as suitable for salads only, but they are quite delicious when quickly wilted under the heat of another item. Toss them with hot pasta or potatoes or pile them on a pizza straight from the oven. Their peppery bite mellows instantly. This is true of salads with hot dressings, as well. Tossing sharply flavored mustard greens with a warm bacon dressing not only wilts the greens but also softens their kick.

Pickling and fermentation: Pickled and fermented vegetables are immensely satisfying ways to enjoy brassicas as a condiment, side dish, or snack. One of the mainstays of Korean cuisine, kimchi is a side dish of seasoned fermented vegetables and is served at nearly every meal. Several types of brassicas are used, such as radishes, bok choy, or, most commonly, napa cabbage. Purchase kimchi at Asian markets or some supermarkets, or try my recipe on page 125. Sauerkraut (page 67) is another great example of fermentation at work. Cauliflower tastes particularly good pickled, as in the vinegary Mexican pickled vegetables on page 50.

Raw: Most of the brassicas can be eaten raw. I have used raw bok choy, cabbage, kale, kohlrabi, arugula, Brussels sprouts, cress, mizuna, tatsoi, tender mustard greens, radishes, and tiny spring turnips in all kinds of fantastic salads. Grated fresh horseradish makes a deliciously punchy salad dressing, and the smallest young collard leaves are perfect for wraps. Many people showcase raw broccoli florets and cauliflower on crudité plates, though I find them both unpleasant to chew and indigestible. If you are using sturdy, fibrous raw leaves such as kale for salads, it is best to shred them finely. If you leave them in large pieces, chewing them will be a challenge.

Keep the Smell Under Control

If you associate cooking cabbage, Brussels sprouts, broccoli, or cauliflower with unpleasantly strong odors, here are some helpful tips to keep down the smell:

Freshness: Choose the freshest vegetables possible and cook them within a few days. When you sniff brassicas at the store, many of them will have a mild cabbagelike scent. It should not be so strong that it is offensive. Brassicas contain sulfur compounds, which means that they will not smell better as they age.

Cooking method: A quick blanch is beneficial in some cases (think broccoli rabe), but continued boiling will transform those sulfur compounds into the trisulfides that will smell up your kitchen. During many months of recipe testing, I found that cooking methods like roasting or sautéing never produced an unpleasant odor. It was only when I used water-based methods, boiling and microwaving specifically, that my family cried foul. Steaming caused fewer issues, but keep the cooking time brief.

Cooking time: The longer the vegetables cook, the more opportunity for their cell walls to break down and release the sulfur compounds. Most brassicas cook in around 15 minutes or less. Any recipe that suggests boiling a brassica for 45 minutes is not going to taste good any way. Do not overcook them.

Leftovers: When you open a container that holds a cooked brassica, you may get that telltale whiff of sulfur. The cell walls of these vegetables were damaged during cooking, which started the release of the sulfur compounds. By containing the vegetables in an enclosed space, especially if the vegetables were still warm, the smell gets trapped. To help with this, make sure the vegetables have cooled completely before packaging leftovers.

Frozen Vegetables

Many brassicas are commonly available frozen, such as broccoli, cauliflower, kale, collards, and Brussels sprouts, to name just a handful. From an economical and convenience standpoint, frozen vegetables are a home run. Because they have already been trimmed and cleaned, there's no waste, essentially making them cheaper (and certainly less work) than purchasing them fresh. But here's the pitfall: frozen vegetables are blanched—that is, precooked—before freezing. This means they are full of water. Most of the recipes in this book would not work well using frozen vegetables, as they are too waterlogged for sautéing, roasting, or salads. If you fancy frozen vegetables, I suggest using them in soups, stews, or other recipes that involve a lot of liquid. Because the vegetables are precooked, keep an eye on the cooking time so they do not get mushy.

Equipment

You do not need a lot of special equipment to cook vegetables. Here are the tools I find myself reaching for repeatedly:

- Large rimmed baking sheets; 18 by 13 by 1-inch pans, known as half sheet pans, are ideal for roasting vegetables

- 12-inch or larger frying pan, one regular and one nonstick

- Steamer insert (a small, collapsible basket type is fine)

- Salad spinner for drying greens

- Large (8-cup) measuring cup for measuring salad greens (a 2-quart pitcher works in a pinch)

- Kitchen scale

- Box grater

- Tongs for tossing salads and wrangling unruly greens

- Chef's knife and paring knife

- Microplane zester

- Stand blender or immersion blender

- Food processor with a slicing attachment or a Benriner slicer (Japanese mandoline)

Pantry Basics

Since a handful of basic ingredients show up again and again throughout this book, I wanted to provide a few more details on some of my pantry staples:

Salt: I developed all of the recipes in this book using Diamond Crystal brand kosher salt. Kosher salt measures differently by volume than fine salt, so if you are using fine sea salt, table salt, or even a different brand of kosher salt, you may want to use less than the quantity listed. I advise starting out by using half the amount indicated and gauge from there. You can always add salt, but you cannot take it away.

Oil: The majority of the recipes call for olive oil, but a neutral-flavored oil is a better fit in some recipes. Whole Foods basic 365 olive oil is a workhorse in my kitchen. I often list canola oil as an option—always choose an organic oil—but you can use a different flavorless oil if you prefer. Grapeseed oil is a good choice.

Broth: Many of the recipes call for chicken or vegetable broth. All of the recipes using broth were tested with chicken broth. I use Pacific or Imagine brand chicken broth because I prefer a gluten-free product, but any high-quality broth is a good choice. I have included vegetable broth to offer a vegetarian option.

Citrus: In recipes that call for both citrus zest and juice, remove the zest from the lemon or lime before cutting into the fruit and juicing it.

Miso Paste: A fermented paste that can range from sweet and mild to salty and pungent, miso is most commonly made from soybeans and rice, though some types include barley or other grains. There are three basic types of miso: white miso is the mildest and sweetest, yellow miso is earthier and lightly salty, and red miso is typically quite salty and strong flavored. Look for miso packaged in small plastic tubs or sturdy bags in the refrigerated section of grocery stores and Asian markets, often near the tofu. It will keep refrigerated for up to 6 months.

Toasted Nuts: Put the nuts in a small frying pan and toast them over medium-low heat, stirring frequently, for 5 to 10 minutes, until golden brown and fragrant. Or, spread them on a rimmed baking sheet and toast them in a 350°F oven for 5 to 10 minutes. Either way, keep a close eye on the nuts to make sure they don't burn. Toasted nuts will keep in an airtight container at room temperature for several days.

curly kale

red russian kale

tuscan kale

No other vegetable has undergone such a dramatic image change as kale, moving from hippie staple to hipster darling seemingly overnight. That new status, which has become almost comically impossible to ignore, led *Bon Appétit* magazine editor-in-chief Adam Rapoport to tweet, "Thinking that if this whole magazine thing doesn't pan out, I should get into kale farming." Whether or not kale deserves its current superstar standing is debatable, but one truth remains: kale is a hearty and satisfying nutritional powerhouse.

Kale leaves have a unique earthy taste, a minerally tang, and a hearty chew. The flavor can be bold, yet it retains a detectable sweetness. The green is not peppery or pungent like some of its brassica cousins, though older leaves or those from plants grown in warmer weather often take on a hint of bitterness. Kale accommodates well to many cooking methods, including sautéing, steaming, roasting, or simmering in soups and stews. It can also be served raw.

Selection

Most grocery stores carry at least one of these kale varieties.

Use the three types interchangeably, unless the recipe specifies one type. Chances are you will eventually choose your own favorite. Always select fresh-looking bunches, avoiding those with droopy, slimy, or yellowing leaves.

Maddeningly, kale bunches range in size from a stingy 6 ounces up to a generous 14 ounces, which makes it impossible to specify the amount you need for a recipe in bunches only. But don't get too frazzled by that. Pop a bunch on the scale in the produce department, and if it seems particularly light, grab a second one. In most recipes, an ounce or two plus or minus won't

Curly kale: Bulky, fluffy bright green leaves with lighter green or whitish stems and thick center ribs.

Red Russian kale: Broad, serrated dark green leaves with purple-tinged edges. The leaves can be flat or curly, with purplish pink stems and ribs.

Tuscan kale (also known as Lacinato, dinosaur, cavolo nero, black, or Italian): Elongated, flat but wrinkled leaves, ranging in color from a dark, rich mineral green to nearly black. Ribs and stems are lighter green.

make much difference. The stems and ribs account for about 30 percent of the weight of the bunch.

Prep

Remove any rubber bands or twist ties from the kale and pop the leaves into a loosely sealed plastic bag. Tuck a paper towel in the bag to absorb any extra moisture and refrigerate the kale for no more than 3 or 4 days. When ready to use, wash the greens (see page 7), and using a V cut, remove the tough center ribs and thick, tough stems (see page 8). Leave the tender, edible stems of small young greens intact. Dry the greens well, especially if they are destined for the salad bowl.

To cut kale into ribbons, stack the leaves in a rough pile—easier with Tuscan flat leaves than unruly curly kale—and cut them crosswise. The recipes will provide specifics, such as "cut into 1/2-inch-wide ribbons," but these are only approximate goals. The size will not make or break the dish, unless you're cutting the kale for a salad. If you will be eating the kale raw, it should be finely shredded. Invariably those who claim to dislike raw kale are the same people who try to gnaw through a whole leaf. To shred kale, stack the leaves and roll them lengthwise into a tight cigar shape. Cut the leaves crosswise as thinly as possible.

Nutrition

Kale is an excellent source of such antioxidant vitamins as K, C, and A and of fiber, lutein, and beta-carotene. It is also high in cancer-preventing glucosinolates and low in calories, at only about 35 per cup.

1 small bunch
= 6 to 8 ounces
= 8 cups loosely packed ribbons

1 average bunch
= 10 ounces
= 10 cups loosely packed ribbons

1 large bunch
= 12 to 14 ounces
= 12 cups loosely packed ribbons

Master Kale Sauté

SERVES 4

2 tablespoons olive oil,
plus more for finishing

4 cloves garlic, minced

1 large or 2 small bunches kale,
center ribs and tough stems
removed, leaves cut crosswise
into ½-inch-wide ribbons
(about 12 cups loosely packed)

Scant ½ teaspoon kosher salt

1 tablespoon water

IF YOU HAVE NEVER SAUTÉED KALE BEFORE, these ultraspecific directions are for you. Of course, all you're really doing is heating the garlic in oil, tossing in the kale, and letting it cook. I prefer flat-leaf Tuscan kale for this recipe, because bulky curly kale takes longer to cook down, but you can choose any kind you like. Some recipes instruct you to blanch kale before you sauté it, a step I consider unnecessary unless you're cooking quite a bit (three bunches or more) and need to fit it all in the pan. If you do decide to blanch the kale, squeeze out any excess water before you sauté it. Use this recipe as a basic side dish, or stir the garlicky kale into a pot of simmering white beans, add it to cooked pasta or to a frittata, or use it as a topping for baked potatoes.

Put the oil and garlic in a large (12 inches or wider), deep frying pan and place over medium-low heat. When the garlic starts to sizzle (do not let it brown), add the kale—a little at a time until all of it fits in the pan—and turn it with tongs to coat it with the oil and garlic. Raise the heat to medium and add the salt and water.

Keep turning the kale with the tongs until it wilts. If the pan seems dry, add another tablespoon water. Keep in mind that you don't want the greens to be overly wet, however. Continue cooking for about 5 minutes, until the kale is tender. If you prefer softer kale, remove the pan from the heat, cover it, and leave to steam for an additional 5 minutes. Taste and finish with a drizzle of oil or additional salt if needed. Serve hot or at room temperature.

VARIATIONS Doctor up this basic side dish with a pinch of red pepper flakes along with the garlic, the grated zest of 1 lemon, a splash of tamari, or a handful of dried cranberries just before removing the pan from the heat, or a couple tablespoons of grated Parmesan cheese, or a scattering of toasted pine nuts just before serving. Or, slice 1 yellow onion and caramelize it in the oil before you add the garlic and kale.

Citrusy Green Smoothie

SERVES 2

¾ cup freshly squeezed orange juice (include pulp)

1¼ cups shredded kale (about 4 leaves)

Large handful of baby spinach leaves (about 1¼ cups)

1 cup diced fresh or frozen pineapple

1 tablespoon agave nectar (optional)

1 tablespoon coconut oil, melted (optional)

1 cup ice

I OFTEN WHIP UP A GREEN SMOOTHIE for breakfast and it keeps me full for hours, especially with the added fat from the coconut oil. If you are new to drinking raw kale, start out with equal parts kale and spinach for a balanced flavor. The orange and pineapple add enough sweetness for me, but if you like a sweeter drink, add the agave nectar. Put the ingredients in the blender in the order listed—juice first, followed by the greens and other ingredients. If you have trouble getting the greens to spin, use a spatula to pat them down into the blender blade—just be sure to turn the blender off first!

Coconut oil is a workhorse in my kitchen, versatile enough to use raw in a smoothie and stand up to high-heat sautéing. I use it not only for its taste—virgin coconut oil smells and tastes tropical; refined versions have a more neutral flavor—but also for its antiviral, antifungal, and antibacterial properties, all of which are due to its high concentration of lauric acid. The oil remains solid at room temperature, liquefying above 75°F. If you need to melt it, as you do for this smoothie, put it in the microwave or set the jar in a pan of hot water. Look for coconut oil in the supermarket near the other types of oil; it's generally packaged in glass or opaque jars.

Put the orange juice, kale, spinach, pineapple, agave nectar, and oil in a blender. Puree for 2 to 3 minutes, until the greens are completely liquefied. Add more juice or a little water if needed. Add the ice and process until finely chopped. Serve immediately.

VARIATIONS Substitute parsley for the spinach, or use a combination of all three greens, to total about 2½ cups. If you like a creamy smoothie, add ¼ cup coconut milk or a scoop of dairy-free coconut ice cream to the blender along with the greens.

THE FIRST TIME I TASTED a raw kale salad, it was a revelation. Although kale puts on a "tough guy" veneer, it can be transformed into an enormously satisfying salad. Wash the leaves first—I use long, flat Tuscan kale here because they are less bulky and slightly more tender than curly kale—and dry them well to avoid diluting the dressing. Raw kale benefits from a little massage to tenderize its fibers. Whether you do this by rubbing the dressing into the leaves with your fingers (kind of fun) or by giving it an extra-thorough toss with tongs is your call. Raw kale also softens after spending some time with an acidic dressing, so don't feel rushed to serve the salad immediately as you would with a soft-leaf lettuce salad.

Feta, a crumbly brine-cured cheese, adds the perfect combination of salty and creamy to this salad. It is made from sheep's milk (or a combination of sheep's and goat's milk), which gives the cheese its notable tanginess. European Union legislation stipulates that only cheeses made in the traditional manner with sheep's milk or a mixture of sheep's and goat's milk in specific areas of Greece may be labeled feta cheese, but similar brine-cured cheeses produced in France, Bulgaria, Denmark, and elsewhere can be substituted here. Indeed, any bright-flavored, salty cheese will shine in this salad. Try an aged goat cheese or grated pecorino (another sheep's milk cheese), though the result will be less creamy.

Lemony Kale Shreds *with* Salty Cheese

SERVES 4

1 large bunch kale (12 to 14 ounces), center ribs and tough stems removed, leaves finely shredded

1 teaspoon Dijon mustard

Grated zest of 1 lemon

2 tablespoons freshly squeezed lemon juice

¼ teaspoon kosher salt

¼ teaspoon freshly ground black pepper

2 tablespoons olive oil

½ cup crumbled feta cheese (about 2 ounces)

Put the kale in a salad bowl. To make the dressing, in a small bowl, whisk together the mustard, lemon zest, lemon juice, salt, and pepper. Add the oil and whisk to combine.

Drizzle the dressing over the kale, then, using your fingertips or tongs, toss together the kale and dressing. Spend a few minutes thoroughly working the dressing into the leaves. (At this point, you can cover and refrigerate the salad for up to 4 hours before serving.) Add the feta and toss once more. Taste and adjust the seasoning with salt or black pepper if needed, then serve.

VARIATION For a dairy-free or vegan dish, add ¹/₂ cup drained, cooked white beans or diced avocado in place of the feta.

Smoky Kale Salad *with* Toasted Almonds *and* Egg

SERVES 4

2 large eggs

Kosher salt

1 large bunch kale (12 to 14 ounces), center ribs and tough stems removed, leaves finely shredded

1 tablespoon sherry vinegar

½ teaspoon smoked paprika (pimentón de la Vera)

¼ teaspoon freshly ground black pepper

3 tablespoons olive oil

⅓ cup sliced almonds, toasted (see page 13)

OVER THE PAST FEW YEARS, raw kale salads have become one of my favorite foods, making it difficult to narrow down which recipes to share. One reason I like them so much is because they take well to all kinds of tasty additions, such as fruits (grapes, dates, figs, pomegranate seeds), nuts (pine nuts, walnuts, almonds, pecans), diced avocado, roasted bell pepper, and aged or salty cheese (goat, feta, Parmesan, pecorino). This salad is particularly straightforward: thinly sliced kale is combined with a Spanish-inspired dressing made from smoked paprika and sherry vinegar and then garnished with chopped egg and toasted almonds. Serve it alone as a simple lunch, or offer it as a side dish to skewers of garlicky grilled shrimp for supper. For an added, albeit expensive, Spanish touch, use Marcona almonds.

Put the eggs in a small saucepan with cold water to cover. Place over medium-high heat and bring to a boil. Remove the pan from the heat, cover, and let stand for 10 minutes. Drain the eggs and then peel them. (You can cook the eggs a day ahead. Keep them covered in the refrigerator.) Chop the hard-boiled eggs into small pieces and toss them with a large pinch of salt.

Put the kale in a salad bowl. In a small bowl, whisk together the vinegar, smoked paprika, ¼ teaspoon salt, and the pepper. Add the oil and whisk to combine.

Drizzle the dressing over the kale, then, using your fingertips or tongs, toss together the kale and dressing. Spend a few minutes thoroughly working the dressing into the leaves. (At this point, you can cover and refrigerate the salad for up to 4 hours before serving.) Add the almonds and eggs and toss once more. Taste and adjust the seasoning with salt and pepper if needed, then serve.

VARIATION To keep with the Spanish theme, shave some aged Manchego cheese over the salad. For a vegan version, omit the egg and add about ⅔ cup roasted red bell pepper strips (jarred is fine; pat them dry) and a few tablespoons golden raisins along with the almonds.

Kale Pesto

MAKES ABOUT 1 CUP

½ cup slivered blanched almonds or pine nuts, toasted (see page 13)

1 clove garlic, smashed

½ teaspoon kosher salt

4 cups loosely packed chopped kale leaves (1 small bunch)

6 tablespoons olive oil

Freshly ground black pepper

I KEEP A STASH OF THIS PESTO in the refrigerator to elevate simple dishes to something special. Spread it on toasted bread and top with diced tomatoes for an easy bruschetta, or toss it with a starchy component—boiled potatoes, cooked white beans, or roasted carrots—for a unique side dish. You can use it as you would basil pesto, as well: add it to hot cooked pasta with a splash of the pasta cooking water. I use Tuscan kale here, but your favorite variety will work.

Put the almonds, garlic, and salt in a food processor. Pulse until the nuts are finely chopped. Add the kale—in batches, if necessary—and pulse until chopped. With the machine running, add the oil through the feed tube in a steady stream; process to a coarse puree. Taste and adjust the seasoning with salt and pepper if needed.

Use the pesto immediately, or store in a tightly sealed container in the refrigerator for 2 to 3 days.

VARIATIONS This vegan version has a clean, mildly bitter flavor. If you prefer a more traditional pesto, add 3 to 4 tablespoons grated Parmesan or pecorino cheese. The cheese will also temper the bitter notes. If you don't care for raw kale, blanch the kale for 1 to 2 minutes to soften its bite, then squeeze out the excess water before adding the kale to the processor.

IF YOU ARE LOOKING FOR A WAY to get your kids to eat kale, this may be the ticket. In fact, the kale chips are so addictive that you should probably make two batches right off the bat (seriously, they go fast!). The trick is to cook the kale at a very low temperature, essentially controlled dehydration. Start off with any type of kale—I like Tuscan, my daughter prefers Red Russian—make sure the leaves are dry, and cut or tear them into similar-size pieces. Spread the kale on rimmed baking sheets—I use 18 by 13-inch pans—and pop them into the oven until the chips are crisp. If you are looking for something more than just a snack, crumble the kale chips over cooked rice or toss a handful into a salad for an interesting contrast of textures.

Roasted Kale Chips

MAKES ABOUT 2 CUPS

1 medium bunch kale (about 10 ounces), center ribs and tough stems removed, leaves cut or torn into smaller, uniform pieces

1 tablespoon olive oil

Scant 1/2 teaspoon kosher salt

Preheat the oven to 300°F. Set the temperature a little lower if you suspect your oven runs hot. Put the kale on a rimmed large baking sheet. Pour the oil over the kale and, using your hands, rub the oil into the kale, making sure each piece is evenly coated. Spread the kale out on the baking sheet in a single layer (you may need 2 baking sheets). Sprinkle the salt evenly over the kale.

Roast the kale for 8 minutes. Remove the pan from the oven, stir the kale, and return the pan to the oven. If are using 2 pans, switch their positions and rotate them back to front. Continue to roast for about 10 minutes more, until the kale is crisp. Peek in the oven during this time to check the progress; you want the kale to dehydrate and crisp, not blacken. When the chips are done, they should be crunchy, not chewy.

Serve the chips immediately, or store in an airtight container at room temperature for up to 3 days.

VARIATIONS Spice up the basic kale chips with one of these great additions: add about 1/2 teaspoon ground cumin, dried oregano, or curry powder, 1/8 to 1/4 teaspoon red pepper flakes, or a splash of red wine vinegar to the kale with the olive oil. To add a cheese flavor, sprinkle a little grated Parmesan or, to keep it vegan, some nutritional yeast flakes (yes, it tastes a bit like cheese) over the chips when you remove them from the oven.

THE SIMPLE COMBINATION of kale, sweet potatoes, and Mexican spices tastes great on its own as a basic side dish, but it can easily work as a main course, as well. I have added a fried egg to each serving to turn it into a breakfast hash and have used it as a taco filling. It also makes a nifty topping for tostadas: pick up tostada shells (crisp corn tortillas) at the grocery store and top them with the sautéed vegetables, chopped fresh cilantro, avocado cubes, and a scattering of crumbled *queso fresco*.

Kale *and* Sweet Potato Sauté

SERVES 4

2 tablespoons olive oil (divided), plus more if needed

1½ pounds sweet potatoes (2 medium), peeled and cut into ½-inch cubes

¾ teaspoon kosher salt (divided)

1 tablespoon chili powder (divided)

1½ teaspoons ground cumin (divided)

2 cloves garlic, minced

1 medium bunch kale (about 10 ounces), center ribs and tough stems removed, leaves shredded

1 tablespoon water

In a large (12 inches or wider) nonstick frying pan, heat 1 tablespoon of the oil over medium heat. Add the sweet potatoes and cook, stirring occasionally, for about 5 minutes, until starting to soften. Stir in ½ teaspoon of the salt, 2 teaspoons of the chili powder, and 1 teaspoon of the cumin. Add a touch more oil if the pan seems dry, then continue cooking, stirring occasionally, for 8 to 10 minutes more, until the sweet potatoes are golden brown and cooked through. If the sweet potato cubes are larger than ½ inch, they may take longer to cook. Transfer the sweet potatoes to a bowl.

In the same pan, heat the remaining 1 tablespoon oil and the garlic over medium heat. When the garlic starts to sizzle (do not let it brown), add the kale—a little at a time until all of it fits in the pan—and turn it with tongs to coat it with the garlicky oil. Add the remaining ¼ teaspoon salt, 1 teaspoon chili powder, and ½ teaspoon cumin. Stir in the water and cook for about 5 minutes, until the kale is wilted and tender. Return the sweet potatoes to the pan and heat for about 2 minutes more, until heated through. Taste and season with salt if needed. Serve hot.

Spicy Kale Fried Rice

SERVES 4

2½ tablespoons plus 1 teaspoon canola or other neutral oil (divided)

2 eggs, beaten with a pinch of kosher salt (optional)

1½ tablespoons peeled, minced fresh ginger (divided)

1 bunch green onions, white and green parts, thinly sliced

1 medium bunch kale (about 10 ounces), center ribs and tough stems removed, leaves finely shredded

½ teaspoon kosher salt (divided)

2 teaspoons Sriracha sauce (divided)

4 cups cooked and chilled rice

1 tablespoon soy sauce or tamari

WHEN COOKING FRIED RICE, I always start with cold cooked rice. I like jasmine rice, but any kind will do. Use leftover rice from a previous meal or pick up an extra quart of plain rice when you order takeout and keep it in the fridge. If you do cook the rice immediately before frying it, spread it out on a baking sheet to cool so that any extra moisture will evaporate. You want fried rice that is firm, not wet and fluffy.

Spicy flavors make a great match for kale. The amount of Sriracha sauce (hot chile sauce) used here is moderate, so you may want to pass the sauce at the table for those who like a spicier dish. Look for Sriracha sauce near the soy sauce in the Asian foods aisle of your grocery store. For a vegan version of this dish, omit the eggs.

Heat a large (12 inches or wider), nonstick frying pan or a wok over medium-high heat. When the pan is hot, add 1 teaspoon of the oil. Then add the eggs and cook, stirring occasionally, for about 1 minute, until scrambled. Transfer the eggs to a large bowl. Raise the heat to high and add 1 tablespoon of the oil, 1 tablespoon of the ginger, and the green onions. Cook, stirring, for about 30 seconds, until fragrant. Add the kale and ¼ teaspoon of the salt and continue to cook, stirring frequently, for 2 to 3 minutes, until the kale is wilted and tender. Stir in 1 teaspoon of the Sriracha sauce and then transfer the vegetables to the bowl with the eggs.

Heat the remaining 1½ tablespoons oil in the pan over medium-high heat. Add the remaining 1½ teaspoons ginger, the rice, and the remaining ¼ teaspoon salt. Cook, stirring occasionally, until the rice is hot, about 3 minutes. Return the vegetables and eggs to the pan and stir to combine. Add the soy sauce and the 1 remaining teaspoon Sriracha sauce and mix well to combine. Taste and adjust the seasoning with soy sauce or Sriracha sauce if needed. Serve hot or at room temperature.

VARIATIONS Use watercress or tatsoi in place of the kale. These greens will likely need to cook for only about 1 minute.

INSPIRATION FOR THIS DISH stems from the fantastic miso-creamed kale at Wafu restaurant (now closed) in Portland, Oregon. Although Wafu's kale dish was an absolute treat, its decadent creaminess was too heavy for me to eat on a regular basis. The flavor combination is brilliant, however, so I increased the amount of mushrooms and kale and substituted a simple sauce of miso and water for the heavy cream–based original. The rethought dish is substantially more healthful, yet equally delicious.

Sake, the popular Japanese alcoholic beverage made from fermented polished rice, is available in many different styles. You'll want a crisp, dry type for this recipe. Look for sake wherever you buy wine. Some shops sell 180-milliliter bottles—about 6 fluid ounces—which are ideal if you typically use only a small amount in cooking. In this recipe, dry vermouth makes an ideal substitute.

Miso-Glazed Kale *and* Shiitakes

SERVES 4

2½ tablespoons canola or other neutral oil (divided)

4 ounces shiitake mushrooms, stems removed, caps thinly sliced (about 2 cups)

1 tablespoon soy sauce or tamari

1 large shallot, sliced

2 medium bunches kale, (about 20 ounces total) center ribs and tough stems removed, leaves cut crosswise into ½-inch-wide ribbons

2 tablespoons sake or dry vermouth

3 to 4 tablespoons water

2 tablespoons white or yellow miso paste (see page 13)

Kosher salt and freshly ground black pepper

In a wide pot or a large (12 inches or wider), deep frying pan, heat 1 tablespoon of the oil over medium heat. Add the shiitakes and cook, stirring occasionally, for about 5 minutes, until softened. Add the soy sauce and stir to coat the mushrooms. Transfer the mushrooms to a bowl.

In the same pan, heat the remaining 1¹/₂ tablespoons oil over medium-low heat. Add the shallot and cook, stirring occasionally, for about 3 minutes, until starting to soften. Add the kale—a little at a time until all of it fits in the pan—and turn it with tongs to coat it with the oil. Continue to cook, stirring occasionally, for about 3 minutes, until wilted. Increase the heat to medium. Add the sake and cook for about 1 minute, until it evaporates. In a small bowl, stir together 3 tablespoons of the water and the miso until smooth. Add it to the pan and cook and stir for about 2 minutes more, until the sauce clings to the kale.

Return the mushrooms to the pan and stir to combine. Taste and adjust the seasoning with salt or a little soy sauce and pepper if needed. Or, if the miso has made the mixture a bit too salty, stir in the remaining 1 tablespoon water. Serve hot.

Sausage, Kale, *and* White Bean Stew

SERVES 4

1 tablespoon olive oil, plus more if needed

12 ounces mild Italian chicken sausage, links or bulk

1 small red bell pepper, diced

1 teaspoon chopped fresh rosemary (optional)

3 tablespoons tomato paste

1 large bunch kale (12 to 14 ounces), center ribs and tough stems removed, leaves cut crosswise into ½-inch-wide ribbons

1 (15-ounce) can white beans (such as Great Northern or cannellini), drained

2½ cups chicken or vegetable broth

¼ teaspoon freshly ground black pepper

2 tablespoons grated Parmesan cheese, plus more for serving (optional)

KALE AND SAUSAGE IS A MATCH MADE IN HEAVEN. In fact, I had to restrain myself from pairing them in every recipe. I enjoy the flavor of chicken sausage here, but high-quality chicken sausage is sometimes hard to find. Pork or turkey sausage—spicy or mild—is a good alternative. A touch of rosemary is optional, but it does add both flavor and anti-inflammatory benefits. If you are on a dairy-free regimen, skip the Parmesan.

In a Dutch oven or other large pot, heat the oil over medium heat. Add the sausage and cook, turning occasionally, for 8 to 10 minutes, until browned and cooked through. If you are cooking bulk sausage, break the meat into large chunks. Using tongs or a slotted spoon, transfer the sausage to a plate.

Return the pot to medium heat. If needed, add oil to the pot to total 1 tablespoon. Add the bell pepper and cook, stirring occasionally, for about 5 minutes, until starting to soften. While the pepper is cooking, if you have used sausage links, cut them into slices.

Add the rosemary and tomato paste and stir to combine. Add the kale— a little at a time until all of it fits in the pot—and turn it with tongs to coat it with the oil. Add the beans, broth, and the cooked sausage and bring to a boil. Lower the heat to a simmer, cover partially, and cook for about 10 minutes, until the kale is tender and the flavors marry. Stir in the black pepper and the Parmesan. Taste and add salt (the need for additional salt will depend on the saltiness of the sausage and broth) and pepper if needed. Ladle into bowls and serve hot with more Parmesan on the side.

VARIATION Use 1 small head savoy cabbage (about 1½ pounds), cored and coarsely chopped, in place of the kale.

Caldo Verde

SERVES 4

1 tablespoon olive oil, plus more if needed

8 ounces to 1 pound kielbasa, quartered lengthwise, then diced

1 yellow onion, thinly sliced

2 cloves garlic, minced

2 pounds Yukon gold potatoes, peeled and cut into 1-inch cubes

1½ teaspoons kosher salt (divided)

4 cups chicken or vegetable broth

2 cups water

1 large bunch kale (12 to 14 ounces), center ribs and tough stems removed, leaves finely shredded

¼ teaspoon freshly ground black pepper

IN THIS BASIC VERSION of the famed Portuguese soup, I substitute an easier-to-find kielbasa for the traditional dry *chouriço* or linguiça sausage. If you have access to these sausages, however, give them a try. (If you are observing a gluten-free diet, check the label on the sausage package, as some contain wheat.) In Portugal, special machines cut the kale into hair-thin shreds, but you can just use a knife and cut the leaves as thinly as possible. The soup's flavor develops as it sits, making it a prime candidate for cooking ahead. The sausage is typically just a garnish, so the amount is small, but you can add up to a pound for a heartier meal.

In a Dutch oven or other large pot, heat the oil over medium-high heat. Add the kielbasa and cook, stirring often, for about 5 minutes, until crisp and browned. Using a slotted spoon, transfer the sausage to a small bowl and set aside.

Return the pot to medium-low heat. If needed, add oil to the sausage drippings to total 1 tablespoon. Add the onion and cook, stirring occasionally, for about 5 minutes, until starting to soften. Stir in the garlic, potatoes, 1 teaspoon of the salt, the broth, and the water. Raise the heat to medium-high and bring to a boil. Turn down the heat to a simmer, cover partially, and cook for about 15 minutes, until the potatoes are tender.

To puree the soup, using a slotted spoon, transfer the solids to a blender and blend until smooth. (Add a little of the liquid if needed to get things moving.) Return the puree to the pot. Alternatively, puree the soup directly in the pot with an immersion blender. Or, if you prefer a chunkier soup, lightly crush the potatoes with a potato masher.

Bring the soup back to a simmer. Stir in the kale, the reserved sausage, and the remaining ½ teaspoon salt. Simmer for about 5 minutes, until the kale is tender. Stir in the pepper. Serve hot or at room temperature with a drizzle of oil.

VARIATION Substitute collard greens for the kale. Be sure the leaves are finely shredded.

THESE INDIVIDUAL FRITTATA "MUFFINS" make a perfect high-protein meal for on-the-go families. They reheat well, so I often make a whole batch early in the morning and then cover and store any leftovers in the refrigerator for up to 2 days. They make great afternoon snacks. But if you prefer to make fewer, use 1 egg plus 3 tablespoons filling for each muffin cup and leave the remaining muffin cups empty. If you do not want to bother cooking bacon, diced salami makes a great alternative.

Preheat the oven to 350°F. Oil 12 muffin cups with olive oil.

In a large frying pan, cook the bacon over medium heat for about 5 minutes, until crisp. Using a slotted spoon, transfer the bacon to a small bowl. Return the pan to medium heat. If needed, add oil to the bacon drippings to total about $1^1/_2$ tablespoons. Add the garlic and when it starts to sizzle (do not let it brown), add the kale—a little at a time until all of it fits in the pan—and turn the kale with tongs to coat it with the garlicky drippings. Stir in $1/_4$ teaspoon of the salt and cook, stirring occasionally, for about 5 minutes, until the kale is wilted and tender. If there is excess liquid in the pan, continue cooking until the pan is dry, as the liquid will dilute the eggs.

Divide the kale, bacon, and red pepper strips evenly among the prepared muffin cups. In a large bowl, whisk together the eggs with the remaining $1/_4$ teaspoon salt and the pepper until well combined. Using a ladle or a measuring cup, divide the eggs evenly among the muffin cups; they should be nearly filled to the top.

To catch spills, put the muffin tin on a rimmed baking sheet and then slip the baking sheet into the oven. Bake for 12 to 15 minutes, until the eggs are puffed and a toothpick inserted into the center of a muffin comes out clean. Serve warm or at room temperature.

VARIATIONS For a vegetarian version, omit the bacon. Instead of pairing the bacon or bell pepper with the kale, try smoked salmon, cooked sausage, diced ham, cubed cooked potatoes, roasted cherry tomatoes, or grated cheese. Anything you would use in an omelet will taste good here.

Kale *and* Egg Muffins
SERVES 4 TO 6

Olive oil, for cooking

4 slices bacon, chopped

1 clove garlic, minced

4 cups finely shredded kale leaves (from one small bunch)

½ teaspoon kosher salt (divided)

¼ cup roasted red bell pepper strips (jarred is fine; pat them dry)

12 eggs

¼ teaspoon freshly ground black pepper

romanesco

CHAPTER TWO

Cauliflower

*yellow, purple, and
white cauliflower*

Poor cauliflower, so underrated, so underappreciated. If your only experience with cauliflower is a crudité plate or a dish of plain boiled florets, you need to give this versatile brassica another chance. When treated properly, cauliflower sings. As noted earlier, the strong tastes (and smells) often associated with inherently mild cauliflower come from overcooking it. Fresh cauliflower tastes nutty and slightly sweet, with a near-neutral palate that welcomes both bold and gentle pairings. Try roasting or sautéing cauliflower to highlight its sweetness. It is also a nutritious lower-carb substitute for potatoes or rice, and even takes on a starchy smoothness when pureed. Plus, because it is white, it is a perfect "sneaker vegetable" to slip the kids.

Selection

Fresh cauliflower looks creamy white and has tight, densely packed florets. It should feel heavy in your hand for its size and be free from blemishes, browning, or wet spots. Any leaves should look fresh and vibrant. Orange, green, and purple cauliflowers (all similar in flavor to white cauliflower) should be uniformly colored and blemish-free. Before you buy, take a whiff of the head. If it has a strong smell, it is likely past its prime and will taste like it when you cook it.

Size is generally not an indicator of quality, so select a cauliflower based on how much you need or what is available.

Romanesco cauliflower, also known as Roman cauliflower and Romanesco broccoli, has a spectacular appearance. The head is a bright lime green and composed of small, tightly wound spiral fractals that are less densely packed than the curds of white cauliflower. Unfortunately, Romanesco can be hard to find, but standard white cauliflower can be used in its place.

Prep

If you purchase cauliflower wrapped in cellophane, free it right away. The cellophane traps moisture that promotes rot. Store whole heads in a loosely sealed plastic bag in the refrigerator for 4 to 7 days; refrigerate precut florets no more than 4 days. Tuck a paper towel in the bag to prevent moisture accumulation.

Cauliflower stalks (peeled and sliced) and leaves (thinly sliced) are edible, so you may consider including them in your cooking. To cut a head of cauliflower into florets, quarter the head through the stem end and cut away the small piece of core from each quarter. Alternatively, flip the cauliflower head upside down, cut around the core with a paring knife, and pull it out like a plug, then quarter the head. Cut the cored cauliflower into bite-size florets. Small florets are ideal because they cook more quickly, and the less time cauliflower cooks, the better it tastes. Rinse the florets and pat them dry before cooking.

As noted above, roasting and sautéing are the best cooking methods for cauliflower. Cauliflower loves salt, so be sure to season it well.

Nutrition

Despite what you have been told about "white foods" lacking nutrition, cauliflower packs a healthful punch. It's high in vitamins C and K, folate, potassium, manganese, fiber, and cancer-preventing glucosinolates. It is also low in calories, with about 25 per cup.

Small head
= $1^1/_2$ pounds
= about 4 cups florets

Average head
= just under 2 pounds
= about 5 cups florets

Large head
= $2^1/_4$ pounds
= about 6 cups florets

Roman Cauliflower Sauté

SERVES 4

3 tablespoons olive oil

1 medium head cauliflower, cored and cut into bite-size florets (about 5 cups)

3 cloves garlic, minced

¾ teaspoon kosher salt

½ teaspoon freshly ground black pepper

3 tablespoon grated pecorino or Parmesan cheese

WHAT YOU WANT TO ACHIEVE HERE is a batch of golden brown florets, which nearly guarantees a satisfying caramelized flavor. Cut the cauliflower into bite-size florets for even, consistent cooking. And when I say "bite size," I mean just that: a piece of cauliflower small enough to eat in a single bite. Sautéing larger chunks tends to be less successful. I love the Roman-inspired combination of garlic, black pepper, and pecorino, but the sauté lends itself to endless variation.

In a large (12 inches or wider) frying pan, heat the oil over medium-high heat. Add the cauliflower, keeping it in a single layer as much as possible. Having a few extra florets is fine, but if they are mounded in a pile, they will not brown or cook evenly. If necessary, use a larger pan, cook them in two batches, or pull out the extra for another use. Cook the florets, stirring occasionally, for about 5 minutes, until they start to brown.

Stir in the garlic and the salt and continue to cook for 3 to 4 minutes more, until the cauliflower is tender but still retains a little bite. If it over-browns (unlikely since you are looking for golden brown), lower the heat to medium. If you prefer softer cauliflower, remove the pan from the heat at this point and cover it to steam for an additional 5 minutes. Stir in the pepper and the cheese. Serve hot or at room temperature.

VARIATIONS Briefly sauté 4 or 5 anchovy fillets, minced, in the oil before adding the cauliflower and omit the cheese. Or, toss in 1/4 cup golden raisins and a few tablespoons each toasted pine nuts and chopped dill along with the cheese for a Sicilian accent. Or, caramelize some onions before adding the cauliflower, and finish the dish with a splash of balsamic vinegar for a sweet-and-sour version. Try adding chopped fresh basil, red pepper flakes, or grated lemon zest near the end of cooking. And don't forget to consider cured pork: a little diced pancetta sautéed in the oil before you add the florets or some strips of sliced prosciutto thrown into the pan at the end dresses up the simple dish nicely.

ONE OF THE FIRST WAYS I truly enjoyed cauliflower was in a dish similar to this one at an Indian lunch buffet. I especially like the textural difference between the cauliflower and the potato, but you could just as easily use 6 or 7 cups cauliflower florets and eliminate the potatoes. The dish is flavored with chile, coriander, cumin, and turmeric. The latter imparts both a vibrant yellow and its potent anti-inflammatory effects to the mix.

Put a large (12 inches or wider), deep frying pan, preferably nonstick, over medium heat. When the pan is hot, add 2 tablespoons of the oil and the ginger and cook, stirring, for about 30 seconds, until fragrant. Add the potatoes, stir to coat with the oil, and cook, stirring occasionally, for 6 to 8 minutes, until the potatoes start to soften.

Add the remaining 1 tablespoon oil, the cauliflower, and $1/2$ teaspoon of the salt and cook, stirring occasionally, for 5 minutes. Stir in the chile, coriander, turmeric, cumin, and the remaining $3/4$ teaspoon salt. Add the water, cover the pan, and then turn down the heat to low. Simmer for 5 to 8 minutes more, until the potatoes and cauliflower are tender. Stir in the peas and cook for about 2 minutes, until heated through. Taste and add additional salt if needed. Stir in the cilantro just before serving. Serve hot or at room temperature.

Indian Potato *and* Cauliflower Curry

SERVES 4

3 tablespoons canola or coconut oil (divided)

1 tablespoon peeled, minced fresh ginger

1½ pounds baking potatoes (about 2), peeled and cut into ½-inch cubes (about 3 cups)

1 small head cauliflower, cored and cut into bite-size florets (about 4 cups)

1¼ teaspoons kosher salt (divided)

1 tablespoon minced jalapeño chile

1 teaspoon ground coriander

1 teaspoon ground turmeric

½ teaspoon ground cumin

2 tablespoons water

½ cup shelled green peas, thawed if frozen

¼ cup chopped fresh cilantro

CAULIFLOWER SHINES when paired with boldly flavored ingredients like capers, mustard, and olives. Here, I combined that zesty trio with olive oil and fresh herbs in a bright *salsa verde*, which I spoon over simply roasted florets. You could sauté the cauliflower instead of roasting it, but slipping it into the oven for a quick roast takes the least amount of effort.

Preheat the oven to 450°F. Put the cauliflower on a baking sheet, drizzle with 2 tablespoons of the oil, sprinkle with 1/2 teaspoon of the salt, and toss to coat evenly, then spread in a single layer.

Roast the cauliflower, stirring once or twice, for about 15 minutes, until golden brown and tender but not mushy. Taste a floret for doneness; larger florets may take slightly longer to cook.

Meanwhile, to make the *salsa verde*, in a small bowl, combine the parsley, chives, capers, mustard, lemon zest, pepper, and the remaining 1/4 teaspoon salt and stir to mix well. Stir in the remaining 4 tablespoons oil and the olives. (The *salsa verde* can be made up to 1 day ahead, covered, and refrigerated until serving.)

Transfer the cooked cauliflower to a serving platter and drizzle the *salsa verde* over the top. Serve hot or at room temperature.

Cauliflower *with* Salsa Verde

SERVES 4

1 medium head cauliflower, cored and cut into bite-size florets (about 5 cups)

6 tablespoons olive oil (divided)

¾ teaspoon kosher salt (divided)

½ cup packed fresh flat-leaf parsley leaves, finely chopped

¼ cup chopped fresh chives

1 tablespoon drained capers, chopped

1 teaspoon Dijon mustard

Grated zest of 1 lemon

¼ teaspoon freshly ground black pepper

8 Cerignola or other large green olives, pitted and coarsely chopped (about ⅓ cup)

Roasted Cauliflower *with* Pickled Peppers *and* Mint

SERVES 4

1 large head cauliflower, cored and cut into bite-size florets (about 6 cups)

2 tablespoons olive oil

¾ teaspoon kosher salt

½ cup hot or sweet pickled peppers, coarsely chopped

⅓ cup chopped fresh mint

¼ teaspoon freshly ground black pepper

3 tablespoons pine nuts, toasted (see page 13), (optional)

Grated Parmesan cheese, for serving (optional)

I TASTED A DISH SIMILAR TO THIS ONE at Girl & the Goat restaurant in Chicago and knew immediately that it was a special way to treat cauliflower. In my version, I roast the florets in a very hot oven until golden brown and then toss them with Mama Lil's pickled peppers, a handful of mint, and some pine nuts. You can use sweet or hot peppers according to your taste, but be sure they are pickled, as the vinegar clinging to the peppers adds bright acidity to the dish. Look for pickled peppers in the condiments aisle of the grocery store near the jarred olives or roasted peppers.

Preheat the oven to 450°F. Put the cauliflower on a rimmed baking sheet, drizzle with the oil, sprinkle with the salt, and toss to coat evenly, then spread in a single layer.

Roast the cauliflower, stirring once or twice, for about 15 minutes, until golden brown and tender but not mushy. Taste a floret for doneness; larger florets may take slightly longer to cook.

Remove the pan from the oven and toss the cauliflower with the pickled peppers, mint, and black pepper. Add the pine nuts and Parmesan and toss again. Taste and add additional salt and pepper if needed. Serve hot.

VARIATION Substitute 2 tablespoons chopped fresh oregano for the mint and add the grated zest of 1 lemon with the oregano.

WHEN CHEF PATRICK FLEMING of Boke Bowl in Portland, Oregon, agreed to share his recipe for this outstanding cauliflower and Brussels sprout salad, I was over the moon. The salad represents everything that chefs are doing right with brassicas, namely celebrating their flavors instead of trying to mask them.

The recipe remains true to the original (though I admit to cutting back on the oil): roast the cauliflower florets and the Brussels sprouts until they are golden brown and then toss them with orange segments and an umami-rich fish sauce vinaigrette.

To make the dressing, in a small bowl, whisk together the fish sauce, water, vinegar, lime juice, sugar, garlic, and chiles. Set aside. (The dressing will keep in an airtight container in the refrigerator for a few weeks.)

Preheat the oven to 400°F. Put the Brussels sprouts on 1 rimmed baking sheet and put the cauliflower florets on a second rimmed baking sheet. Drizzle each vegetable with 2 tablespoons of the oil, sprinkle each with $1/2$ teaspoon of the salt, and toss to coat evenly, then spread in a single layer.

Roast the vegetables, stirring once or twice, for 10 to 15 minutes, until golden brown and tender but not mushy. The cauliflower and Brussels sprouts may cook at different rates. Remove them from the oven as they are finished cooking.

While the vegetables are roasting, section the orange: Using a medium-size sharp knife, cut a thin slice off the top and bottom of the orange to expose the flesh. Stand the orange upright on a cutting board. Following the contour of the fruit, cut downward to remove the peel, white pith, and thin membrane in wide strips, rotating the orange as you work. Holding the orange in your nondominant hand, and using a paring knife, cut along both sides of each section to free it from the membrane, letting the sections fall onto the cutting board. Dice the sections.

Transfer the warm vegetables to a bowl, add the orange segments and vinaigrette, toss well, and serve warm.

VARIATIONS In the summer, chef Fleming substitutes broccoli florets for the Brussels sprouts and uses $1/2$ cup cubed mango in place of the orange. To garnish the salad with Brussels sprouts leaves, blanch the leaves in boiling water for 30 seconds, then plunge them in ice water to stop the cooking, drain, and pat dry.

Boke Bowl Cauliflower *and* Brussels Sprout Salad *with* Thai Vinaigrette

SERVES 4

2 tablespoons Asian fish sauce

1 tablespoon warm water

1 tablespoon unseasoned rice vinegar

2 tablespoons freshly squeezed lime juice

1 tablespoon sugar

1 clove garlic, minced

1 teaspoon minced serrano or, for a less spicy dish, jalapeño chile

3 cups halved Brussels sprouts (about 1 pound), or substitute broccoli florets

3 cups bite-size cauliflower florets (about 12 ounces)

4 tablespoons olive oil (divided)

1 teaspoon kosher salt (divided)

1 orange (preferably a blood orange or Cara Cara), or substitute ½ cup diced mango

Cauliflower

Creamy Cauliflower Gratin

SERVES 6

2 cups vegetable or chicken broth

1 medium head cauliflower, cored and coarsely chopped (about 5 cups)

1 cup plain Greek yogurt (2 percent or full fat)

1½ teaspoons Dijon mustard

2 teaspoons kosher salt

½ teaspoon freshly ground black pepper

½ cup shredded Gruyère or Fontina cheese (2 to 3 ounces)

¼ cup grated Parmesan cheese

3 small shallots, thinly sliced (optional)

⅔ cup sliced almonds, coarsely chopped

ALMOST NOTHING IS MORE DELICIOUS than a bubbling cauliflower gratin, flowing with cream and cheesy goodness. I wanted to keep the homey feel of the dish while lightening it up enough to eat it on a regular basis, so I cooked the cauliflower in broth for flavor and then mashed it with Greek yogurt and a touch of mustard—no cream in sight. To achieve a crisp crust without weighing the gratin down with bread crumbs, try chopped sliced almonds. Gratin recipes often call for cups and cups of cheese, but by using the highly flavorful combination of Gruyère and Parmesan, I have kept the quantity reasonable.

Preheat the oven to 375°F. Oil or butter a 12 by 8-inch baking dish.

In a saucepan, combine the broth and cauliflower over medium-high heat and bring to a boil. Turn down the heat to medium-low, cover, and simmer, stirring occasionally, for 10 to 15 minutes, until completely tender. Drain the cauliflower well in a colander and return it to the pot.

Add the yogurt, mustard, salt, and pepper to the cauliflower and coarsely mash the mixture with a potato masher or a fork. (For a smoother puree, use a handheld mixer.) Transfer the mashed cauliflower to the prepared baking dish. Scatter the cheeses and shallots evenly over the cauliflower. (You can prepare the dish to this point up to a day ahead. Cover and refrigerate until ready to bake, then add 10 to 15 minutes to the baking time.) Sprinkle the nuts evenly over the top.

Bake the gratin for about 25 minutes, until the top is golden. Serve hot.

Cauliflower Soup *with* Gingerbread Spices

SERVES 4 TO 6

2 tablespoons unsalted butter or canola oil

1 small yellow onion, thinly sliced

1 medium head cauliflower, cored and coarsely chopped (about 5 cups)

2 apples, peeled and diced, with peels reserved for garnish

1¾ teaspoons kosher salt, more if needed

¾ teaspoon ground cinnamon (divided)

½ teaspoon ground ginger

5 whole cloves

4 cups chicken or vegetable broth

1 teaspoon honey

MY FRIENDS Jennifer Bryman and Mollie Dickson started a fabulous organization called The Heart's Kitchen, which educates and empowers expectant and new moms to eat and cook nutritious foods for their children's lifelong health. This soup—cauliflower paired with sweet apples and warm gingerbread spices—is a perfect example of the healthful yet family-friendly style of cooking the group promotes. The soup purees to such a surprisingly smooth consistency that your kids will think they are eating potatoes. And while the color isn't a showstopper (you could choose a yellow cauliflower if you can find one), the clever apple peel garnish adds a splash of color to your bowl. Choose a sweeter variety of apple, such as Gala, Fuji, Braeburn, or Golden Delicious, for the soup.

In a large pot, melt the butter over medium-low heat. Add the onion and cook, stirring occasionally, for 8 to 10 minutes, until soft. Do not let the onion brown. Add the cauliflower, apples, salt, ½ teaspoon of the cinnamon, the ginger, cloves, and broth and bring to a boil. Lower the heat to a simmer and cook, partially covered, for about 20 minutes, until the apples and cauliflower are tender.

While the soup is cooking, prepare the garnish: Cut the apple peels into fine shreds and put them in a bowl. Add the honey and the remaining ¼ teaspoon cinnamon and toss to coat evenly. Cover with plastic wrap and set aside until needed.

Remove the soup from the heat and let cool slightly, then remove and discard the whole cloves. Puree the soup in a blender, in batches if necessary, until smooth. Gently reheat the soup to serving temperature. (Alternatively, puree the soup directly in the pot with an immersion blender.) Taste and add additional salt if needed. Ladle into bowls and top each serving with the apple peel garnish. Serve hot. (The soup can be prepared up to two days ahead, covered, and refrigerated until ready to reheat. The garnish, however, will brown quickly. Make a fresh garnish or skip it altogether.)

VARIATION For a vegan version, substitute a neutral-flavored oil for the butter, use vegetable broth, and replace the honey with agave nectar.

IN AN EFFORT TO INCORPORATE vegetables into snacks as well as meals, I whipped up this kid-friendly hummus with only cauliflower, tahini, and a few seasonings. Use it as a dip for carrots, celery, or tortilla chips; roll it up in slices of salami for *involtini*; or slather it on bread as a sandwich spread. Because I steam rather than boil the cauliflower, the texture of the hummus is thick and rich rather than grainy. You can even use frozen cauliflower here, but shorten the cooking, as frozen cauliflower is partially cooked. If the steamed cauliflower is very wet, roll it up in the clean kitchen towel and squeeze it lightly to remove more water before continuing with the recipe. Look for tahini, a creamy puree of sesame seeds, in the supermarket near the peanut butter.

Cauliflower Hummus

MAKES ABOUT 3 CUPS

4 cups coarsely chopped cauliflower (about 1 small cauliflower)

1 small clove garlic, smashed

⅓ cup well-stirred tahini

3 tablespoons olive oil

2 tablespoons freshly squeezed lemon juice

1 teaspoon kosher salt

Scant ¼ teaspoon cayenne pepper

¾ cup tightly packed fresh cilantro leaves

Set up a collapsible steamer basket in a large pot over (not touching) an inch or two of water and bring the water to a boil. Put the cauliflower in the basket, cover the pot, and steam for about 5 minutes, until tender. (Alternatively, put the cauliflower in a microwave-safe bowl, add 3 to 4 tablespoons water, cover with plastic wrap, and microwave until tender.) Spread the cauliflower on a clean kitchen towel to remove excess water and cool to room temperature.

Transfer the cauliflower to a food processor and pulse until finely chopped. Remove the lid and scrape down the side of the bowl. Add the garlic, tahini, oil, lemon juice, salt, and cayenne and process until the hummus is thick and smooth, stopping once or twice to scrape down the sides of the bowl. Add the cilantro and process until chopped. Taste and add more salt if needed.

Serve chilled or at room temperature. The hummus will keep in an airtight container in the refrigerator for up to 2 days.

Romanesco Summer Salad

SERVES 4

1 cup water

1 medium Romanesco or regular cauliflower, cored and cut into bite-size florets (about 5 cups)

2 teaspoons whole-grain Dijon mustard

Grated zest of 1 lemon

2 tablespoons freshly squeezed lemon juice

¾ teaspoon kosher salt (divided)

3 tablespoons olive oil

1 red bell pepper, chopped

½ cup thinly sliced red onion

⅓ cup chopped fresh dill

3 tablespoons drained capers, coarsely chopped

ALTHOUGH VIBRANT LIME GREEN ROMANESCO (sometimes called broccoli Romanesco or Romanesco cauliflower) looks like the love child of cauliflower and broccoli, it is actually closer to cauliflower in terms of taste and how it is used. Its color is fantastic in this lively salad, though you can definitely use white cauliflower if that's all you can find. Cook the Romanesco just long enough to take away the raw bite, 2 to 3 minutes tops. Normally I would suggest plunging the florets into ice water to halt the cooking immediately, but introducing extra water here will mute the flavor and dilute the dressing. Instead, cook them fast and then spread them on a baking sheet so they cool quickly.

In a large pot, bring the water to a boil over high heat. (If you have a steamer insert, put it in the pot to hold the Romanesco. If you don't have one, don't worry about it.) Add the Romanesco, cover the pot, turn down the heat to medium, and steam for 2 to 3 minutes, until crisp-tender. Using a slotted spoon, transfer the Romanesco to a rimmed baking sheet or clean kitchen towel, spreading it in a single layer, to cool.

In a small bowl, to make the vinaigrette, whisk together the mustard, lemon zest, lemon juice, and ¼ teaspoon of the salt. Slowly add the oil, whisking constantly with a fork to form an emulsified vinaigrette.

Put the Romanesco in a serving bowl. Add the bell pepper, onion, dill, capers, the remaining ½ teaspoon salt, and the vinaigrette and toss gently to combine. Cover and refrigerate until ready to serve. It will keep well for several hours. Just before serving, taste and add more salt if needed.

Mexican Pickled Vegetables

MAKES ABOUT 6 CUPS

3 cups water

6 cloves garlic, halved lengthwise

3 bay leaves

1½ teaspoons dried oregano leaves (not powdered)

1 teaspoon black peppercorns

1 medium head cauliflower, cored and cut into bite-size florets (about 5 cups)

1 pound carrots (about 6), peeled and sliced into ¼-inch-thick coins

2 teaspoons kosher salt

3 jalapeño chiles, pierced in several places with the tip of a knife or halved lengthwise

3 tablespoons olive oil

2 cups unseasoned rice vinegar

I AM ALWAYS EXCITED when I sit down in a Mexican restaurant to a bowl of *zanahorias en escabeche*, or "pickled carrots." It crossed my mind that cauliflower might taste similarly wonderful pickled, and indeed it does. Use the pickles as a condiment or a crunchy snack alongside sandwiches, chili, or Mexican food. Be sure to pierce the jalapeños with the tip of a knife to infuse their spiciness into the pickling liquid. You could also halve them lengthwise, which will yield a considerably spicier pickle. I prefer to use mildly acidic rice vinegar (be sure to use plain rice vinegar, not one that contains sugar and salt), but I have seen versions that use cider vinegar or distilled white vinegar, too. You're welcome to experiment.

In a saucepan, combine the water, garlic, bay leaves, oregano, and peppercorns and bring to a boil over high heat. Add the cauliflower, carrots, and salt and cook for about 3 minutes, until crisp-tender. Add the chiles, oil, and vinegar and return the liquid to a boil. Remove from the heat and let cool to room temperature.

Using a slotted spoon, transfer the vegetables to Mason jars or other containers with tight-fitting lids. Ladle the pickling liquid over the vegetables, submerging them completely. Cover and refrigerate for at least 24 hours to develop the flavor before serving. The pickles will keep refrigerated for up to 2 weeks.

I WAS SKEPTICAL when I started to hear about serving cauliflower "rice" as a low-carb alternative to real rice, but now that I've tried it, I'm a fan. It cannot be an exact replica, of course, but its similar mouthfeel produces an impressive and healthful substitute. This version creates a neutral- and mild-flavored dish, better suited to being a bed for a Thai curry or a spicy stir-fry than standing alone. It also distantly resembles couscous, which makes it a nice match for a Moroccan *tagine* (stew). Or try it as a replacement for bulgur in an herb-flecked tabbouleh.

Cauliflower Rice

SERVES 4

1 medium head cauliflower (about 2 pounds), cored and cut into large florets

⅓ cup water

½ teaspoon kosher salt

Olive oil, for drizzling (optional)

Put half of the cauliflower in the bowl of a food processor and pulse until the cauliflower resembles rice. Transfer the cauliflower to a saucepan. Repeat with the remaining cauliflower and add to the pan. (If you do not have a food processor, grate the cauliflower on the large holes of a box grater.)

Add the water and salt to the pan and bring to a simmer over medium heat. Cover the pan, turn down the heat to medium-low, and steam for 10 to 12 minutes, until the cauliflower is just tender. Check from time to time to make sure the water has not cooked away. If the pan looks dry, add more water as needed, 1 tablespoon at a time. You want enough water to get the steaming started but not so much that the cauliflower is waterlogged. When the cauliflower is tender, taste and add more salt and a drizzle of oil if needed. Serve hot.

VARIATION I prepare cauliflower rice as described, pulsing it first and then steaming it. But you can also reverse the steps and steam it first and then pulse the cooked cauliflower in the food processor until it resembles rice. Do not overprocess or you'll end up with a puree. You can also steam the cauliflower in the microwave, though I find it smells up the kitchen.

green cabbage   Brussels sprouts

CHAPTER THREE

Brussels Sprouts and Cabbage

red cabbage

The history of the Brussels sprout is a bit fuzzy. Although its origin may lie in the Mediterranean, it takes its name from a northern European capital, Brussels, Belgium, a city where it was reportedly known as early as the thirteenth century. Some folks regard Brussels sprouts as "baby cabbages," which they are not, though they do have a similar flavor profile and can be used in similar ways. When young sprouts are cooked properly, they have a cabbagelike flavor tinged with a sweet nuttiness. Overcooked, their flavor and their smell becomes unpleasantly pungent.

Cabbage shares a similar story, sweet and mild when lightly cooked yet unappealing when it has spent too long on the stove. Its crisp texture also makes it an ideal vegetable for serving raw in salads.

Selection

When choosing Brussels sprouts, smaller is better. Larger sprouts have a stronger flavor, plus they tend to overcook if you try to cook them whole. Select small, tightly closed, uniform orbs with evenly green leaves that show no sign of yellowing. Brussels sprouts are typically sold either loose or prepackaged in netting or pint-size containers. If you happen to come across the sprouts still attached to their stalk, give them a try.

Choose cabbages with tightly closed heads that feel heavy for their size. The leaves should look fresh, with no yellowing or brown spots. Fresh green or red (purple) cabbage leaves are smooth and thick; savoy leaves range from light to vibrant green and have a crinkly texture. Napa cabbage is discussed in chapter seven with the other Asian brassicas.

Prep

If you purchased Brussels sprouts in a cellophane-wrapped pint container, transfer them to a loosely sealed plastic bag. They will keep refrigerated for up to 3 or 4 days. Tuck a paper towel in the bag if moisture starts accumulating. If the sprouts came packaged in netting, refrigerate them as is.

When you are ready to cook the sprouts, rinse them, then trim the ends with a paring knife and remove the outer layer or two of leaves if they are less than perfect. Unless the sprouts are truly tiny (an inch or less wide), don't cook them whole. Efforts to cook large Brussels sprouts uniformly are likely to result in overcooking. Get creative with the cutting: halve or quarter them through the stem end, shred them, or separate the head into individual leaves. Roast, sauté, or lightly steam sprouts to highlight their sweetness, making sure not to cook them beyond crisp-tender. Unless the sprouts are tiny, do not boil them, as the method does not bring out their best qualities.

Purchase whole heads of cabbage. Red and green cabbages are widely available but savoy is less so. Do not confuse savoy cabbage with napa cabbage. Both have crinkly leaves, but the former is round and the latter is oblong and has a significantly higher water content. Whole heads of red or green cabbage will keep in the produce drawer of your refrigerator for up to a couple weeks. Savoy cabbage is more perishable but will keep for a week or perhaps a bit longer. Once you cut into a whole head, refrigerate the remainder in a loosely closed plastic bag for about a week. Tuck a paper towel in the bag to prevent moisture accumulation.

When you are ready to use the cabbage, discard any outer leaves that lack freshness. Halve or quarter the cabbage through the stem end and cut out the core with a paring knife. Rinse halved cabbage under running water, or wash shredded or chopped cabbage as you would leafy greens (see page 7) and dry well, especially if it is destined for the salad bowl. Lay the cabbage flat side down on the cutting board before slicing or chopping it. The weight of a cabbage head can vary dramatically, so I also offer cup measurements when appropriate. Keep in mind that cabbage is more delicate than it appears and thus shines with quick cooking.

Nutrition

Brussels sprouts are high in fiber, folate, magnesium, potassium, and vitamins A, C, and K. Like most brassicas, they are full of cancer-preventing glucosinolates. Brussels sprouts contain about 40 calories per cup.

Cabbage is a great source for vitamins C and K, fiber, B_6, and the anti-inflammatory amino acid glutamine. It is extremely low in calories, about 22 per cup.

1 pound Brussels sprouts
= about 4 to 5 cups halved Brussels sprouts
or 8 cups shredded Brussels sprouts or 10 cups loosely packed Brussels sprouts leaves

1 small cabbage
= about 1 3/4 pounds

1 medium cabbage
= 2 pounds

1 large cabbage
= 2 1/2 pounds or larger

Roasted Brussels Sprouts *with* Parmesan Crust

SERVES 4

1½ pounds Brussels sprouts, trimmed and halved through the stem end (about 6 cups)

2 tablespoons olive oil

½ teaspoon kosher salt

¼ teaspoon freshly ground black pepper

⅓ cup plus 3 tablespoons shredded Parmesan cheese

1 teaspoon white wine vinegar

EVEN THOUGH IT TAKES almost no effort at all, roasting produces some of the tastiest Brussels sprouts you'll ever eat. The high heat works quickly on the sprouts, leaving you with a tray full of golden brown goodies in only minutes. When you are cutting the Brussels sprouts in half, don't worry if their leaves start to separate. In fact, consider this a bonus. The roasted leaves char and crisp around the edges and end up being the most memorable bites.

Preheat the oven to 400°F. Put the Brussels sprouts on a rimmed baking sheet, drizzle with the oil, sprinkle with the salt and pepper, and toss to coat evenly, then spread in a single layer. Roast for 10 minutes. Add the ⅓ cup cheese to the Brussels sprouts and stir to combine. Continue to roast for about 10 minutes more, until the Brussels sprouts are tender and well browned.

Transfer to a serving bowl, add the vinegar and the remaining 3 tablespoons cheese, and toss. Serve warm or at room temperature.

VARIATION Use balsamic vinegar in place of the white wine vinegar. An aged balsamic vinegar works especially well here.

AFTER TESTING THIS RECIPE multiple times to determine the best way to cut the Brussels sprouts, separating the sprouts into individual leaves emerged as the clear winner. Steaming the sprouts whole or even halved left the salad too chunky. The leafy version, billowy and as light as air, gives the creamy dressing a chance to cloak every bite. Admittedly, separating the leaves is a huge pain, but it goes much faster if you halve or quarter the sprouts first. (When you get down to the core, you can thinly slice it and include it in the dish.) If you prefer not to separate the leaves, halve the sprouts through the stem end, turn the halves flat side down, and cut lengthwise into thin shreds with the knife. Alternatively, use a food processor fitted with the slicing blade to slice the halved sprouts thinly. The dressing also works well with other brassicas (see variations).

Brussels Sprout Leaves *with* Lemony Yogurt Dressing

SERVES 4

Scant 1 cup plain Greek yogurt (2 percent or full fat)

1 small clove garlic, minced

Grated zest of 1 lemon

2 tablespoons freshly squeezed lemon juice

1 tablespoon olive oil

1 teaspoon kosher salt (divided)

¼ teaspoon freshly ground black pepper

1 pound Brussels sprouts, trimmed

⅓ cup chopped fresh mint or flat-leaf parsley

⅓ cup shelled unsalted pistachios, chopped (optional)

To make the dressing, in a small bowl, stir together the yogurt, garlic, lemon zest, lemon juice, oil, 1/2 teaspoon of the salt, and the pepper, mixing well. Cover and refrigerate until ready to use. (The dressing will keep refrigerated for up to 2 days.)

Cut each Brussels sprout into halves through the stem end, then separate the halves into leaves. You should have about 10 loosely packed cups leaves. Set up a collapsible steamer basket in a large pot over (not touching) an inch or two of water and bring the water to a boil. Put the leaves in the basket, cover the pot, and steam for about 2 minutes, until just tender. Transfer the cooked leaves to a clean kitchen towel to remove excess water and let cool to room temperature.

Transfer the leaves to a serving bowl and toss with the remaining 1/2 teaspoon salt and half of the dressing. Add the mint and as much of the remaining dressing as you like. (You may use more or less dressing, depending on how you sliced the sprouts.) Gently combine with a spatula. Serve immediately at room temperature or chill, covered, for up to 2 hours. Top with the pistachios just before serving.

VARIATIONS The lemony yogurt dressing works equally well with a pound of lightly steamed broccoli florets or broccolini cut into 2-inch lengths. Drain the steamed vegetables on a kitchen towel to avoid diluting the dressing. Or, even easier, shred raw green or savoy cabbage (not napa cabbage; it is too soft) and coat it with the dressing for an interesting slaw.

Charred Brussels Sprouts *with* Pancetta *and* Fig Glaze

SERVES 4

3 tablespoons olive oil (divided)

3 to 4 ounces pancetta, diced

1½ pounds Brussels sprouts, trimmed and halved (or quartered if large) through the stem end (about 6 cups)

¼ teaspoon kosher salt

2 tablespoons fig jam

1 tablespoon water

¼ teaspoon freshly ground black pepper

NOTHING TASTES BETTER with Brussels sprouts than cured pork, which is why I unapologetically offer you recipes that flavor sprouts with both pancetta and bacon (page 61). Here, the salty pancetta plays well with the sweetness from the fig jam, and you can finish the dish with a drizzle of balsamic vinegar to add a tangy note (see variations). I found fig jam near the grocery store's cheese counter (not in the jams and jellies aisle), but you could also try apricot or peach jam instead. You may want to add a touch more jam than I suggest, but strive for a subtle sweetness rather than a cloying, sticky mess.

In a large (12 inches or wider) frying pan, heat 1 tablespoon of the oil over medium heat. Add the pancetta and cook, stirring occasionally, for about 3 minutes, until crisp. Using a slotted spoon, transfer the pancetta to a small bowl. Return the pan to medium-high heat and add the remaining 2 tablespoons oil. Add the Brussels sprouts, keeping them in a single layer as much as possible. Having a few extra sprouts is fine, but if they are mounded in a pile, they will not brown or cook evenly. If necessary, use a larger pan, cook them in two batches, or pull out the extra for another use. Stir in the salt. Cook, stirring occasionally, for about 10 minutes, until the Brussels sprouts are tender and well browned—even charred in spots. If the sprouts are browning too quickly, lower the heat to medium.

Add the fig jam and the water and stir until the jam melts and coats the Brussels sprouts. Add the reserved pancetta and the pepper and stir to combine. Taste and add additional salt or pepper if needed. Serve warm.

VARIATIONS For a sweet, salty, tangy version, add a drizzle (a teaspoon or less) of balsamic vinegar at the end. Aged balsamic is an especially good choice. Although I prefer pancetta here (I like its unsmoked rich pork flavor), you can use bacon in its place.

Keralan-Style Brussels Sprouts

SERVES 4

6 tablespoons shredded
unsweetened dried coconut

2 tablespoons water

1 pound Brussels sprouts

2 tablespoons coconut oil or
canola oil

1 teaspoon brown or black
mustard seeds

1 teaspoon ground cumin

¾ teaspoon kosher salt

½ teaspoon ground turmeric

½ teaspoon red pepper flakes

I FIRST TRIED *thoran*, an intriguing and unusual vegetable dish from the state of Kerala, in India, with cabbage, but gambled that Brussels sprouts might make a great alternative. Traditionally, the preparation involves quickly cooking chopped vegetables with coconut, fresh curry leaves, and a mix of spices. Because curry leaves, a common ingredient in southern Indian cooking, can be difficult to find unless you live near an Indian market, I have made sure this version tastes just as delicious without the leaves.

In a small bowl, combine the coconut and water and set the bowl aside.

Trim the ends off the Brussels sprouts. Halve the sprouts through the stem end, turn each half flat side down, and cut the halves into shreds. Alternatively, use the slicing blade on the food processor to shred the halved sprouts. (Be sure to use the slicing blade, not the shredding blade, which will shred them too finely.) You should have about 8 cups.

In a large (12 inches or wider), deep frying pan or a wok, heat the oil with the mustard seeds over medium-high heat. Cook for about 3 minutes, until the seeds start to sizzle. Stir in the Brussels sprouts, cumin, salt, turmeric, and red pepper flakes and cook, stirring frequently, for about 3 minutes, until the sprouts wilt.

Add the coconut mixture and cook for 1 to 2 minutes more, until the Brussels sprouts are just tender. Taste and add additional salt if needed. Serve hot or at room temperature.

VARIATIONS Substitute 4 cups finely chopped green or savoy cabbage for the Brussels sprouts. If you do find curry leaves (no relation to curry powder), which are dark green, similar in shape to California bay leaves, and have an intoxicating aroma, toss about a dozen of them into the pan along with the mustard seeds.

HERE IS ANOTHER RECIPE in which I finely shred the Brussels sprouts. I actually find the repetitive motion of cutting them by hand satisfying, but you can speed up the work by using a food processor with the slicing blade. Because the onion here is cooked in the bacon fat, you want to serve the salad while it is warm; cooled bacon fat has an unpleasant mouthfeel.

Trim the ends off the Brussels sprouts. Halve the sprouts through the stem end, turn each half flat side down, and cut the halves into shreds. Alternatively, use the slicing blade on the food processor to shred the halved sprouts. (Be sure to use the slicing blade, not the shredding blade, which will shred them too finely.) You should have about 8 cups.

In a large (12 inches or wider), deep frying pan, cook the bacon over medium heat for about 5 minutes, until crisp. Using a slotted spoon, transfer the bacon to a small bowl. Return the pan to medium-low heat. If needed, add oil to the bacon drippings to total about 3 tablespoons. Add the onion and cook, stirring occasionally, for about 5 minutes, until wilted.

Add the mustard and vinegar to the pan, stir well, and bring to a simmer. Stir in the Brussels sprouts, the 1 tablespoon oil, salt, pepper, and reserved bacon. Turn the Brussels sprouts with tongs to coat them with the dressing and cook for about 2 minutes, until barely wilted. Stir in the cherry tomatoes. Serve warm.

VARIATION For a vegan version, omit the bacon and use 3 tablespoons olive oil in place of the bacon drippings. You may need additional salt and/or pepper for flavor.

Wilted Brussels Sprouts *with* Bacon *and* Tomatoes

SERVES 4

1 pound Brussels sprouts

4 ounces thick-sliced bacon, cut crosswise into narrow strips

Olive oil, as needed for cooking, plus 1 tablespoon

1 small red onion, diced

2 teaspoons Dijon mustard

Scant ⅓ cup cider vinegar

¾ teaspoon kosher salt

¼ teaspoon freshly ground black pepper

¾ cup quartered cherry tomatoes

Colcannon *with* Brussels Sprout Leaves

SERVES 4

2 pounds Yukon gold potatoes, peeled and quartered

2 cups chicken or vegetable broth

12 ounces Brussels sprouts, trimmed and quartered, then separated into leaves (about 7 cups loosely packed leaves)

1 bunch green onions, white and green parts, cut into 1-inch lengths (optional)

2 tablespoons unsalted butter, at room temperature

1¼ teaspoons kosher salt

WHEN IT COMES DOWN TO IT, the traditional Irish dish known as col-cannon is simply mashed potatoes with leafy vegetables. It typically combines rich mashed potatoes with either kale or cabbage, but I took liberties and used Brussels sprout leaves. In an effort to lighten the dish, I simmered the Brussels sprouts and green onions in broth and then used that same broth to mash the potatoes. If you want to make mashed potatoes according to your favorite recipe and stir the greens in at the end, that's fine, too. As you separate the leaves from the Brussels sprouts, you will likely be left with a bit of core. You can discard it or chop it and simmer it along with the leaves. If separating the leaves sounds too labor-intensive, halve and shred the sprouts instead or try the kale or cabbage variations.

Put the potatoes in a medium saucepan, add water to cover, and bring to a boil over high heat. Turn down the heat to a simmer and cook for 15 to 20 minutes, until tender. Drain well and then return the potatoes to the pan.

While the potatoes are cooking, bring the broth to a simmer in a saucepan. Add the Brussels sprout leaves and green onions and cook for about 3 minutes, until just tender. Using a slotted spoon, transfer the vegetables to a bowl. Reserve the broth.

Using a potato masher (or use your favorite method), mash the butter and salt into the hot potatoes. Pour about 1/2 cup of the reserved broth into the potatoes and then incorporate it using a wooden spoon or a spatula. Add as much of the remaining broth as needed until the potatoes have the desired consistency. Stir in the reserved vegetables, then reheat over low heat if necessary. Serve hot.

VARIATIONS Substitute 4 cups shredded green or savoy cabbage or kale leaves in place of the Brussels sprouts. For a vegan version, use vegetable broth and a butter substitute. Or, omit the butter and whisk in a touch of olive oil for richness.

WHEN CHOPPED ROMAINE AND CUCUMBERS start to feel boring, create a new-style Greek salad with shaved Savoy cabbage and thinly sliced fennel. Punch up the bright dressing by adding plenty of fresh herbs: dill, parsley, mint, or a combination should do the trick. And if you are lucky enough to purchase fennel with the wispy fronds still attached, you can chop them and use them as part of the herb mix. I enjoy the sweet delicacy of savoy cabbage, but regular green cabbage works, as well.

Greek Shaved Cabbage *and* Fennel Salad

SERVES 4

To shave the cabbage, cut out the core with the tip of a knife and place the cabbage cut side down. Cut the cabbage lengthwise (through the stem end) as thinly as possible. You should have about 6 cups shaved cabbage.

In a large serving bowl, whisk together the vinegar, mustard, salt, pepper, and lemon juice. Whisk in the oil to form an emulsified vinaigrette. Add the cabbage, fennel, and green onions and toss until the vegetables are well combined with the dressing. Chill the salad, covered, for up to 3 hours, or serve it right away.

Just before serving, add the olives, feta, and herbs and toss to mix. Taste and add additional salt and pepper if needed.

VARIATION Add salami slices, cut into narrow strips, to create a light main-course salad.

½ head savoy or green cabbage (about 1 pound)

3 tablespoons red wine vinegar

1 teaspoon Dijon mustard

½ teaspoon kosher salt

½ teaspoon freshly ground black pepper

1½ tablespoons freshly squeezed lemon juice

¼ cup olive oil

1 large fennel bulb, trimmed, quartered lengthwise, thinly sliced crosswise (about 2 cups)

1 bunch green onions, white and green parts, thinly sliced

½ cup pitted and coarsely chopped Cerignola or other large green olives

½ cup crumbled feta cheese

⅓ cup chopped fresh dill, flat-leaf parsley, and/or mint

Five-Spice Red Cabbage Salad

SERVES 4 TO 6

1 small red cabbage (about 1¾ pounds)

¼ cup mirin

1½ teaspoons kosher salt

1½ teaspoons Chinese five-spice powder

2 tablespoons olive oil

1 bunch green onions, white and green parts, thinly sliced

1 avocado, halved, pitted, peeled, diced, and tossed with a large pinch of kosher salt

½ cup sliced almonds, toasted (see page 13)

MY FRIEND SARAH has a special way with red cabbage, whether it is her sweet-and-sour Swedish Christmas version or this unique Asian-inspired salad. The flavor comes from a combination of mirin, a syrupy cooking wine made from glutinous rice (which is, incidentally, gluten free), and Chinese five-spice powder, a blend that contains star anise, cinnamon, fennel, and more. The mirin adds sweetness and mild acidity to the dish. I prefer Takara brand mirin, which I find in the Asian foods aisle in the grocery store. Look for the five-spice powder in the same place or in the spices aisle, or use your favorite curry powder. If you use a larger cabbage than the recipe calls for, be sure to adjust the amount of seasonings accordingly.

To chop the cabbage, halve the head through the stem end, cut out the core with the tip of the knife, and place the halves cut side down. Cut the halves into about 1/4-inch-thick slices, rotate the slices 90 degrees, and cut across the slices to create roughly 1/4-inch pieces. You should have about 8 cups.

In a large bowl, toss the cabbage with the mirin, salt, and five-spice powder. Let the salad stand for at least 15 minutes at room temperature, or for up to 2 hours in the refrigerator if you plan to serve it chilled; the cabbage will start to wilt.

Add the oil, green onions, avocado, and almonds to the cabbage. Toss gently with tongs to combine. Taste and add additional salt or mirin if needed. Serve chilled or at room temperature. The salad will wilt as time passes. Eat it within a few hours for the most crunch.

Braised Sauerkraut *with* Apples *and* Cider

SERVES 4

2 tablespoons olive oil

1½ teaspoons cumin seeds

2 Granny Smith or other tart apples, peeled and thinly sliced

3 cups drained sauerkraut, store-bought (from a 1½-pound jar) or homemade (page 67)

1½ cups apple cider

½ teaspoon freshly ground black pepper

NO DISCUSSION OF CABBAGE feels complete without acknowledging sauerkraut, one of its most celebrated—and healthful—dishes. Sauerkraut is a rich source of probiotics and beneficial enzymes and bacteria to aid digestion and is high in vitamin C. I am going out on a limb and guessing that you do not want to make your own sauerkraut (though you could, as it is not hard; see page 67). Fortunately, it is easy enough to find in supermarkets or natural foods stores. For the best quality, look for fresh sauerkraut in the refrigerated section; avoid the canned versions. I like Bubbies brand, which is traditionally fermented using only salt, water, and cabbage. If the sauerkraut you find contains vinegar or other ingredients, give it a quick rinse and drain it well before using it in this recipe. This cumin-and-apple-laced sauerkraut is a little sweet, kind of tangy, and a great accompaniment to kielbasa or thick slices of ham. Be sure to save a big spoonful for tomorrow's Reuben.

Put the oil and the cumin seeds in a large (12 inches or wider), deep frying pan and place over medium heat. When the seeds start to sizzle, add the apples and cook, stirring occasionally, for about 2 minutes, until starting to soften. Stir in the sauerkraut and cider and bring to a simmer. Adjust the heat to maintain a simmer, cover partially, and cook for about 15 minutes, until the apples are just tender.

If more than a little liquid remains, uncover the pan and simmer vigorously for a few more minutes to reduce the liquid. (This is a matter of personal preference, however. If you like more liquid, you can leave it.) Stir in the pepper. Serve hot or at room temperature. The sauerkraut will keep, tightly covered, in the refrigerator for up to 3 days. Reheat before serving.

Homemade Sauerkraut

MAKES 1 QUART

Put the cabbage in a large bowl and add the salt. (If you use more than 2 pounds of cabbage, add more salt as well, about $1/2$ teaspoon per pound of cabbage.) Using your hands, work the salt into the cabbage, squeezing and pressing the cabbage for 2 minutes or more, until it starts to wilt and release some liquid.

Transfer the cabbage and any liquid to a noncorrosive container, such as a ceramic crock, a large glass jar, or a food-grade plastic container. Pack the cabbage tightly in the container. Cover loosely with a clean kitchen towel and let stand at room temperature for 4 hours.

Press the cabbage down firmly to condense it—I use a potato masher for this—and note the level of the liquid. The cabbage must be completely submerged to prevent mold from forming. If the cabbage is not submerged, add brine (1 teaspoon kosher salt to 1 cup water) as needed to cover. Weight down the cabbage to keep it submerged—for example, top it with a small plate or a ziplock plastic bag filled with water—and cover the container with an airtight lid.

Let the cabbage stand at room temperature to ferment. Check it once a day to make sure it remains submerged and that no scum appears on the surface. (If scum does appear, scrape it off and discard it.) After about 4 days, start tasting the sauerkraut; taste it every few days until it is fermented to your liking. This should take 7 to 10 days. At this point, the sauerkraut can be refrigerated for up to 2 months. As you remove sauerkraut from the jar, tightly pack down the remaining kraut to keep it submerged in the brine.

1 medium head green cabbage (2 pounds total), quartered, cored and finely shredded (about 12 cups)

$1 1/4$ teaspoons kosher salt (do not use iodized salt)

Roasted Cabbage Wedges *with* Lemon-Thyme Vinaigrette

SERVES 4

1 medium head green cabbage (about 2 pounds)

4 tablespoons olive oil (divided)

¾ teaspoon kosher salt (divided)

2 tablespoons freshly squeezed lemon juice

1 teaspoon chopped fresh thyme

½ teaspoon freshly ground black pepper

LOOKING FOR A RIDICULOUSLY EASY side dish? You won't find anything much easier than cutting a cabbage into wedges and popping the wedges into the oven! You can eat the cabbage straight from the oven, but I like to boost the flavor with a drizzle of lemony vinaigrette. Or, you can add toppings—nuts, bacon, or cheese—and serve as a warm wedge salad.

Heat the oven to 425°F. Cut the cabbage into 8 wedges through the stem end, keeping some core attached to each wedge so the leaves do not separate. Put the cabbage wedges on a rimmed baking sheet. Pour 2 tablespoons of the oil over the cabbage and turn the wedges to distribute the oil evenly. Sprinkle ½ teaspoon of the salt evenly over the wedges. Roast the cabbage, turning once at the midway point, for 30 to 35 minutes, until golden brown and tender.

Meanwhile, to make the vinaigrette, in a small bowl, whisk together the lemon juice, thyme, the remaining ¼ teaspoon salt, and the pepper. Whisk in the remaining 2 tablespoons oil.

When the cabbage is ready, remove from the oven and drizzle the vinaigrette over the wedges. Serve hot or at room temperature.

VARIATIONS Substitute fresh rosemary or oregano for the thyme. Sprinkle chopped walnuts, crumbled cooked bacon, or crumbled feta or soft goat cheese over the cabbage for a warm salad.

Cabbage Confetti Quinoa

SERVES 4

½ small head red cabbage (scant 1 pound)

2 tablespoons unsalted butter or canola oil

2 large cloves garlic, minced

1 tablespoon peeled, minced fresh ginger

1 red bell pepper, cut into small dice

½ teaspoon ground turmeric

¾ teaspoon kosher salt (divided)

2 cups cooked ivory quinoa (see recipe)

WHEN MY FRIEND KYRA feels under the weather, her husband, Jason, whips up a batch of quinoa and cabbage as "comfort food" to speed her healing (much more healthful than my comfort food, tapioca pudding). If you can, start with chilled cooked quinoa—leftovers from the fridge are perfect—since freshly cooked quinoa is a bit too moist here. Otherwise, cook a batch of quinoa and let it cool before adding it to the pan. This dish tastes amazing with just the vegetables and spices, too, so you can skip the quinoa altogether and enjoy the colorful "confetti" by itself.

To chop the cabbage, cut out the core with the tip of a knife and place the cabbage cut side down. Cut into about ¼-inch-thick slices, rotate the slices 90 degrees, and cut across the slices to create roughly ¼-inch pieces. You should have about 4 cups.

Put the butter, garlic, and ginger in a large (12 inches or wider), deep frying pan over medium-high heat. When the garlic and ginger start to sizzle, add the bell pepper and cook, stirring occasionally, for about 3 minutes, until starting to soften. Add the cabbage, turmeric, and ½ teaspoon of the salt and cook, stirring frequently, for about 3 minutes, until the cabbage wilts. (The cabbage is perfectly delicious at this point. If you like, skip the quinoa and eat the dish now.)

Stir in the quinoa and the remaining ¼ teaspoon salt. Cook, stirring frequently, for about 2 minutes more, until hot. Taste and add additional salt if needed. Serve hot or at room temperature.

Quinoa

MAKES 2 CUPS

1¼ cups water

¾ cup ivory quinoa, rinsed

In a small saucepan, bring the water to a boil over high heat. Stir in the quinoa, cover the pan, turn down the heat to low, and cook for about 12 minutes, until a spiral white "tail" appears at the center of each grain. Remove from the heat, fluff the quinoa with a fork, re-cover, and let stand for about 5 minutes. To use the quinoa right away, spread it on a rimmed baking so that it cools quickly. If you have cooked it in advance, let cool, cover, and refrigerate. It will keep for up to 3 days.

SOMETIMES A SIMPLE BOWL of vegetable soup bridges the gap between bone-chilling cold and cozy warmth. Leeks and savoy cabbage add a subtle sweetness here, but yellow onions and green cabbage would do a fine job, as well. I always save the rinds from my Parmesan cheese (you can freeze them) and then simmer them in the broth for added flavor and body. I have even purchased the rinds—very inexpensively—from the cheese counter at my local grocery store. Don't worry if you have leftovers, as the soup tastes even better the next day.

To shred the cabbage, cut out the core with the tip of a knife and place the cabbage cut side down. Cut the cabbage lengthwise (through the stem end) into approximately 1/8-inch-wide slices. You should have about 6 cups shredded cabbage.

In a soup pot, heat the oil over medium heat. Add the leeks and carrot and cook, stirring occasionally, for about 5 minutes, until starting to soften. Add the cabbage and salt and cook for about 2 minutes, until the cabbage has wilted.

Add the tomatoes with their juice, oregano, broth, water, and Parmesan rind, raise the heat to high, and bring to a boil. Turn down the heat to a simmer, cover partially, and cook for 10 to 15 minutes, until the cabbage is tender. Stir in the beans and simmer for about 5 minutes more, until heated through.

Remove and discard the Parmesan rind if possible (otherwise avoid eating it). Stir in the pepper. Ladle into bowls and serve hot. Pass the grated Parmesan at the table.

VARIATIONS Substitute shredded kale for the cabbage. You could also include sliced zucchini or diced potatoes in the soup (add them along with the cabbage). Or, for a thick minestrone-like soup, boil about 1/2 cup pasta (elbows or small shells) in a separate saucepan, drain, and add to the soup with the beans.

For a vegan soup, use vegetable broth and omit the cheese rind and the grated cheese.

Rustic Vegetable Soup
SERVES 4

1/2 head savoy or green cabbage (about 1 pound)

3 tablespoons olive oil

2 leeks, white and light green parts, halved lengthwise and thinly sliced crosswise

3 carrots, peeled, halved lengthwise and thinly sliced

2 teaspoons kosher salt

1 (15-ounce) can diced tomatoes, with juice

2 teaspoons dried oregano or basil leaves (not powdered)

4 cups chicken or vegetable broth

1 cup water

1 Parmesan cheese rind, approximately 4 by 2 inches (optional), plus grated Parmesan for serving

1 (15-ounce) can white beans (such as Great Northern or cannellini), drained

1/4 teaspoon freshly ground black pepper

broccoli   broccolini

Broccoli

broccoli sprouts

Broccoli stirs up strong emotions. It seems that you either love it or hate it. If you grew up eating plain steamed broccoli or, even worse, raw broccoli and dip, you need to broaden your menu. Broccoli does have a prominent flavor, though it can also be delightfully grassy and even rather sweet. It appreciates strong companions—blue cheese or spicy red curry paste, for example— though even milder partners are good additions. You will be amazed by the magic a little garlic, red pepper flakes, and salt can conjure.

The best way to enjoy broccoli is to cook it. Raw broccoli is extremely hard to digest, though you can soften its fibers by marinating sliced stalks or tiny florets in an acidic dressing. Try roasting, sautéing, lightly steaming, or grilling it. Skip boiling broccoli, which too often results in a mushy and unpleasant batch of overcooked florets and invariably infiltrates your kitchen with a sulfurous odor.

Broccolini has a flavor profile similar to that of broccoli, but with comparatively thin edible stalks and loose, open florets. Most broccoli recipes focus on florets, but broccolini, also known as baby broccoli, is really all about the stalks. You can substitute broccolini for regular broccoli, though it more closely resembles Chinese broccoli (see chapter six).

Selection

Broccoli is widely available and often you have a choice: broccoli crowns or crowns with long stalks attached. Although it favors cooler weather, you can find it year-round. Choose broccoli with densely packed, tightly closed florets and firm, nonwoody stalks. Colors range from dark green to green with a bluish or purple tint. Avoid broccoli crowns with yellowing florets or rotting wet spots.

It is hard to specify exact weights for a "head" of broccoli, since it can be sold with or without stalks, bundled into bunches, or wrapped in cellophane. If you don't have a kitchen scale at home, weigh the broccoli in the produce department to get a sense of its heft.

Choose broccolini with long, thin stalks and clusters of loose florets. The color should be bright green, with no yellowing or wilting. Broccolini is sold in small bundles that generally range from 6 to 12 ounces.

Prep

If the broccoli is packed in cellophane, remove it right away. The cellophane can trap moisture, which can cause rot. Store broccoli in a loosely sealed plastic bag. Whole heads will keep in the refrigerator for 4 to 7 days; store precut florets for no more than 4 days. Tuck a paper towel in the bag to prevent moisture accumulation.

When ready to cook, using a sharp knife, trim about 1 inch from the base of the stalk, separate the stalk from the florets—the crown—and cut the crown into individual florets. Surprisingly, many cooks discard the broccoli stalks (or stems), which are quite delicious. To prepare the stalks for cooking, peel away the tough outer layer (about $1/8$ inch deep) with a paring knife until you reach the lighter-colored, juicy, crisp center, then thinly slice or dice them. If you plan to cut the broccoli into long spears for grilling or roasting, peel the stalk without detaching it from the crown. Rinse the broccoli in cool water or, if you suspect a problem with aphids, soak it in cold salted water for about 15 minutes and then rinse it well.

To prepare broccolini, trim off about $1/2$ inch from the end of each stalk. The stalks should be quite thin, so they do not require peeling. Rinse the broccolini well before cooking.

Nutrition

Broccoli is rich in calcium, potassium, and magnesium; is a fantastic source of vitamins C, A, and K; and is rich in fiber and folate. It is also high in glucosinolates, which help the body rid itself of toxins and may reduce the risk of contracting certain types of cancer. Broccoli sprouts are particularly healthful (see page 95). Like most brassicas, broccoli is low in calories, with only about 30 per cup.

Steam-Sautéed Broccoli

SERVES 4

2 tablespoons olive oil

2 cloves garlic, thinly sliced

1¼ pounds broccoli, crowns cut into bite-size florets and stalks (if using) peeled and diced (about 6 cups), florets and stalks reserved separately

½ teaspoon kosher salt

3 tablespoons chicken or vegetable broth or water

WHEN MY SISTER REQUESTED that I include this recipe for "really tasty broccoli," I admit I felt a little surprised. This is the type of dish I throw together without even thinking about it. That said, it is also one that every cook should keep in his or her back pocket. You can use the same technique for other types of vegetables—leafy greens, green beans, even asparagus. I use a splash of chicken broth to get the steam going, since it adds both moisture and flavor. You can use water instead, but you may need to add an extra pinch of salt to compensate.

Put the oil and garlic in a large (12 inches or wider), deep frying pan and place over medium heat. When the garlic starts to sizzle, add the broccoli stalks and cook, stirring, for about 1 minute.

Add the broccoli florets and salt and stir to coat the florets with the garlicky oil. Cook for about 3 minutes, until the broccoli turns bright green. Add the broth, turn down the heat to medium-low, cover, and steam for about 5 minutes, until the broccoli is tender. If you prefer softer broccoli, add a few minutes to the steaming time. Taste a floret and add additional salt if needed. Serve hot or at room temperature.

I WILL NEVER UNDERSTAND why people throw away broccoli stalks. My favorite part of the vegetable, they retain a crisp juiciness that you never find in the florets. You can include the stalks in any recipe that calls for broccoli, but sometimes I like to hoard them for a dish like this one. For ease, choose fat stalks if possible—less peeling, higher yield of inner stem—and save the florets for another use. Kohlrabi, another member of the brassica family, complements the broccoli in this combination. If you cannot find kohlrabi, try one of the variations.

Kohlrabi *and* Broccoli Stalk Slaw

SERVES 4

1¼ pounds broccoli stalks (about 6 fat stalks)

1 pound kohlrabi bulbs (about 3)

2 tablespoons soy sauce or tamari

1 tablespoon unseasoned rice vinegar

1 tablespoon canola or other neutral oil

1½ teaspoons toasted sesame oil

½ teaspoon peeled, grated fresh ginger

¼ teaspoon red pepper flakes

¼ cup chopped fresh cilantro

Using a paring knife, trim about 1 inch off the bottom of each broccoli stalk and then peel off the tough outer layer, cutting about ⅛ inch deep. The inner stalk should appear lighter in color, fresh, and juicy. Cut the stalks crosswise into thin slices, no more than ⅛ inch thick. You should have about 2 cups.

Similarly, cut away the tough outer layer of each kohlrabi bulb with the knife. (If there are fresh leaves attached, save them to steam or stir-fry them with a bit of soy sauce.) Cut each kohlrabi into thin slices. Stack the slices and cut them into matchstick strips. You should have about 2 cups.

In a serving bowl, combine the soy sauce, rice vinegar, canola oil, sesame oil, ginger, and red pepper flakes. Add the vegetables and toss to coat them with the dressing. Cover and refrigerate for at least 1 hour to soften the broccoli stalks and give the flavors a chance to meld. (The salad tastes best when made an hour or two ahead of serving. After that, the vegetables start to release liquid that dilutes the dressing.) Toss in the cilantro just before serving. Serve chilled or at room temperature.

VARIATIONS Try matchstick strips of peeled daikon radish in place of the kohlrabi. Squeeze them to release excess liquid before adding to the dressing. Or, use 4 cups of either sliced broccoli stalks (you will need to stockpile a lot of stalks for this version) or kohlrabi matchstick strips, which is less labor-intensive, instead of using both vegetables. Add other vegetables to the slaw, like julienned carrots, red bell pepper strips, or tiny steamed broccoli florets. Finish the dish with a sprinkle of toasted sesame seeds. Or, purchase a bag of "broccoli slaw"(julienned broccoli stalks) in the produce section near the coleslaw. Simply mix the dressing as directed and toss in the broccoli slaw. The taste will not be as fresh as the version you cut yourself, but it is quick.

THIS COMBINATION OF broccoli and chickpeas makes an ideal side dish, but you can easily turn it into a main dish, as well. Mix the chop with cooked quinoa or rice and toasted pine nuts, or toss it with cooked pasta shells and Parmesan cheese. Don't worry about cutting the broccoli into dainty florets; just put it on the cutting board (peel the stalks first, if using) and chop away until you have a big, green mound. Tarragon adds a unique twist to the dish, but you can substitute fresh chives or even basil if you prefer.

Put the oil and garlic in a large (12 inches or wider), deep frying pan and place over medium heat. When the garlic starts to sizzle, add the chickpeas and stir to coat them with the garlicky oil. Add the broccoli and salt and cook, stirring occasionally, for about 2 minutes, until the broccoli turns bright green. Stir in the water, turn down the heat to medium-low, cover, and cook for 5 minutes.

Lift the lid and give the broccoli a stir. If the pan seems dry, add another 1 tablespoon water. Re-cover the pan and continue to steam for 2 to 3 minutes more, until the broccoli is tender. Stir in the pepper, lemon zest, lemon juice, and tarragon, then taste and add additional salt, pepper, and lemon juice if needed. Serve hot or at room temperature.

Lemony Broccoli Chop

SERVES 4

3 tablespoons olive oil

2 cloves garlic, minced

1 (14 to 15-ounce) can chickpeas, drained and rinsed

1 pound broccoli, finely chopped (about 5 cups)

1 teaspoons kosher salt

2 tablespoons water

¼ teaspoon freshly ground black pepper

Grated zest of 2 lemons

1 tablespoon freshly squeezed lemon juice

1 tablespoon chopped fresh tarragon, or 2 tablespoons chopped fresh chives

Grilled Broccoli *with* **Mustard Vinaigrette** *and* **Blue Cheese**

SERVES 4

1 pound broccoli

1½ tablespoons red wine vinegar

1¼ teaspoons Dijon mustard

¼ teaspoon kosher salt

¼ teaspoon freshly ground black pepper

3 tablespoon olive oil

⅓ cup crumbled blue cheese (about 1½ ounces), such as Rogue Creamery's Smokey Blue

A HEARTY SIDE DISH of grilled broccoli is a perfect accompaniment to burgers or a grilled steak. If you have a grill screen (mine is stainless steel), set it on top of the grill grate to keep the broccoli from slipping through the gaps. Purchase whole heads of broccoli, that is with stalks and crowns attached, so that you can cut the vegetable into long spears.

Using a paring knife, trim about 1 inch off the bottom of each broccoli stalk and then peel off the tough outer layer, cutting about ⅛ inch deep. The inner stalk should appear lighter in color, fresh, and juicy. Cut the broccoli heads into long spears about ¼ to ½ inch wide.

In a bowl large enough to hold the broccoli, whisk together vinegar, mustard, salt, and pepper, then whisk in the oil to make a vinaigrette. Remove 1 tablespoon of the vinaigrette and put it in a small bowl; set aside. Add the broccoli to the large bowl and toss it with the vinaigrette until well coated. Set aside until ready to cook.

Prepare a medium-hot fire in a charcoal or gas grill. Place the broccoli directly onto the grate or a grill screen and grill, turning frequently, for 8 to 10 minutes, until crisp-tender and lightly charred. (If you want the broccoli to be softer, use a medium fire and cover the grill.)

Transfer the broccoli to a platter. Drizzle with the reserved vinaigrette and then top with the cheese. Serve hot or at room temperature.

VARIATIONS Instead of grilling the broccoli, roast it for 10 to 12 minutes in a 425°F oven. You can substitute broccolini for the broccoli in either case.

TOSSING BROCCOLI WITH OLIVE OIL and salt and popping it into a hot oven to roast makes a perfectly acceptable side dish, but I wanted to add a little pizzazz. A savory granola does just that: toast some rolled oats and nuts with a bit of seasoning, stir in some golden raisins, and then sprinkle the combo over the broccoli for added crunch and flavor. You can play with the granola by adding some chopped fresh rosemary or thyme (about 1 teaspoon), or swapping out the golden raisins for dried cranberries. (If you are following a gluten-free diet, make sure the oats are certified gluten-free.) Be sure to cut the broccoli into bite-size pieces so the granola does not get lost in a forest of giant green trees. And if 1½ pounds of broccoli sounds like too much for your family dinner—I can polish off the whole platter by myself—just roast a little less and toss it with the same amount of granola.

Roasted Broccoli *with* Savory Granola

SERVES 4

¼ cup old-fashioned rolled oats

¼ cup coarsely chopped walnuts

3 tablespoons olive oil (divided)

¾ teaspoon kosher salt (divided)

¼ teaspoon freshly ground black pepper

⅓ cup golden raisins

1½ pounds broccoli, cut into bite-size florets

Preheat the oven to 350°F. In a small baking dish, stir together the oats, walnuts, 1 tablespoon of the oil, ¼ teaspoon of the salt, and the pepper. Bake the granola, stirring once or twice, for about 15 minutes, until golden brown. Remove the granola from the oven and stir in the raisins. (The granola can be made several days ahead. Let cool and store in an airtight container at room temperature until ready to use.)

Raise the oven temperature to 425°F. Put the broccoli on a baking sheet, drizzle with the remaining 2 tablespoons oil, sprinkle with the remaining ½ teaspoon salt, and toss to coat evenly, then spread in a single layer. Roast the broccoli, stirring occasionally, for 10 to 15 minutes, until browned and tender.

Transfer the broccoli to a serving bowl and sprinkle the granola over the top. Serve warm or at room temperature.

Broccoli

Broccoli *and* Pepper Jack Frittata

SERVES 4

2 tablespoons olive oil

2 cloves garlic, minced

2 cups bite-size broccoli florets (about 8 ounces)

¾ teaspoon kosher salt (divided)

2 tablespoons water

6 eggs

¼ teaspoon freshly ground black pepper

1 cup shredded pepper Jack cheese (3 to 4 ounces)

THE DAY I STOPPED THINKING of vegetables as just a "dinner thing," my vegetable consumption skyrocketed. This broccoli frittata, for example, works equally well as a healthy breakfast, a simple lunch alongside a green salad, or cut into strips as a party appetizer. It tastes good at room temperature and reheats well, too, so you can nosh on leftovers for an afternoon snack. Pepper Jack melts well and has tons of flavor, but you can substitute another cheese with less of a kick.

Preheat the oven to 400°F. Put the oil and garlic in a 10- to 12-inch non-stick frying pan and place over medium heat. When the garlic starts to sizzle, add the broccoli, stir to coat it with the oil, and cook for about 2 minutes. Stir in ¼ teaspoon of the salt and the water and cook, stirring occasionally, for about 5 minutes, until the broccoli is tender.

Meanwhile, in a bowl, beat the eggs with the remaining ½ teaspoon salt and the pepper until blended. When the broccoli is ready, sprinkle the cheese evenly over it and then add the eggs to the pan. Cook for about 2 minutes, until the eggs are set around the edges.

Transfer the pan to the oven (if the handle of the pan is not ovenproof, wrap it in a few layers of aluminum foil) and bake for 8 to 10 minutes, until the eggs are just set. A knife inserted into the frittata should come out clean. Remove from the oven and carefully slide the frittata out onto a serving plate. Serve warm or at room temperature.

VARIATIONS If you are not a fan of pepper Jack, try another flavorful melting cheese, such as Fontina or smoked mozzarella. You can substitute cauliflower florets for the broccoli, and while you are at it, fry some diced bacon or pancetta along with the cauliflower.

Creamy Leek *and* Broccoli Soup

SERVES 4

2 tablespoons olive oil

3 leeks, white and light green parts, halved lengthwise and thinly sliced crosswise

1½ teaspoons kosher salt (divided)

3 cloves garlic, peeled but left whole

6 cups broccoli florets and peeled, diced stalks (about 1½ pounds)

3½ cups chicken or vegetable broth

Freshly ground black pepper, for serving

Chopped fresh chives, for serving (optional)

MANY SOUPS GET THEIR CREAMY TEXTURE from loads of dairy—cream, sour cream, cheese—or by incorporating a starch such as cooked rice or potatoes. I have found that pureeing broccoli and leeks with a small amount of broth yields a thick, satisfying soup that highlights the pure flavor of the vegetables. I always include the peeled broccoli stalks in the soup, but you can use only florets if you prefer. Although I like the simplicity and pure vegetable flavor of the pureed broccoli and leeks, you can add richness by swirling in a tablespoon or two of butter at the end or by topping each serving with a touch of grated cheese or crumbled cooked bacon. My tasting team suggests serving a grilled cheese sandwich alongside this soup.

In a large pot, heat the oil over medium-low heat. Add the leeks and ¹/₂ teaspoon of the salt, cover, and cook, stirring occasionally, for about 10 minutes, until wilted. Stir in the garlic, broccoli, and the remaining 1 teaspoon salt. Pour in the broth, raise the heat to medium-high, and bring to a boil. Lower the heat to a simmer, partially cover, and cook for about 10 minutes, until the broccoli is tender.

Remove from the heat and let cool slightly. Transfer the soup to a blender, in batches if necessary, and puree until smooth. Gently reheat the soup to serving temperature. Alternatively, puree the soup directly in the pot with an immersion blender. (The soup can be prepared up to 2 days ahead, covered, and refrigerated until ready to reheat.)

Ladle the soup into bowls, top with some pepper and chives, and serve hot.

EVERY ONCE IN A WHILE I make traditional Thai soups using authentic ingredients like lemongrass, kaffir lime leaves, fresh chiles, galangal, and more. But when I need a quick version, I turn to prepared curry paste for flavor. Pick up red curry paste (I like Thai Kitchen brand), along with coconut milk and fish sauce, in the Asian foods aisle of almost any grocery store. Once you have the ingredients on hand, this soup comes together quickly. The soup is a bit spicy. If that makes you wary, start with a little less curry paste or serve some jasmine rice alongside to tame the heat.

Red Curry Soup
with Broccoli *and* Shrimp

SERVES 4

1 (14 to 15-ounce) can coconut milk

¼ cup Thai red curry paste

3 cups chicken or vegetable broth, or more if needed

1 small yellow onion, sliced

3 tablespoons Asian fish sauce

2 tablespoons brown sugar

4 cups bite-size broccoli florets (about 12 ounces)

1 pound medium raw shrimp, peeled and deveined

3 tablespoons freshly squeezed lime juice

⅓ cup chopped fresh cilantro

Sriracha or other hot chile sauce, for serving (optional)

Pour the coconut milk into a saucepan and whisk in the curry paste. Place over medium heat and bring to a simmer, whisking occasionally. Stir in the broth and onion and return the liquid to a simmer. Add the fish sauce, brown sugar, broccoli, and shrimp, stir well, and simmer for about 5 minutes, until the broccoli is tender and the shrimp are cooked. Taste the soup, and if it is too spicy for you, stir in a little more broth.

Remove from the heat and stir in the lime juice and cilantro. Ladle into bowls and serve hot.

VARIATION If you do not eat shrimp, substitute cubes of firm tofu or additional vegetables, such as small whole or halved mushrooms or sliced red bell peppers.

Broccoli

MY FRIEND DANIELLE CENTONI, Portland, Oregon, food writer and editor of *Mix* magazine, showed up at a potluck one day with a roasted broccolini dish similar to this one. When I asked Danielle if she would share the recipe, she responded in a way that made me chuckle: "It's very loosey-goosey. I used what I had around." I rarely pay attention to quantities when I am throwing something together at home, either, but with Danielle's guidance—and excellent memory—we were able to piece together what she had done. The broccolini tastes great at room temperature, so you can cook it ahead of time, or you can make the mushroom sauce while the vegetables are roasting.

Roasted Broccolini *with* Winey Mushrooms

SERVES 4

1½ pounds broccolini (2 large bunches), ends trimmed

4 tablespoons olive oil (divided)

1 teaspoon kosher salt (divided)

1 small sweet onion, finely diced

8 ounces cremini or other mushrooms, thinly sliced

¼ cup dry white wine or vermouth

¼ teaspoon freshly ground black pepper

Grated Parmesan cheese, for serving (optional)

Preheat the oven to 400°F. Put the broccolini on a baking sheet, drizzle with 2 tablespoons of the oil, sprinkle with ¹/₂ teaspoon of the salt, and toss to coat evenly, then spread in a single layer. Roast the broccolini, turning once with tongs, for 10 to 15 minutes, until crisp-tender. If the broccolini stems are not uniform in size, remove thinner ones as they are done. Transfer the broccolini to a platter. (The broccolini can be cooked several hours ahead of time and kept at room temperature.)

In a large (12 inches or wider) frying pan, heat the remaining 2 tablespoons oil over medium heat. Add the onion and cook, stirring occasionally, for about 5 minutes, until starting to soften. Raise the heat to medium-high, add the mushrooms and the remaining ¹/₂ teaspoon salt, and cook, stirring occasionally, for 7 to 10 minutes, until the mushrooms are golden brown. (The mushrooms will release a lot of liquid before reabsorbing it and browning. Be patient, as the flavor is in the browning.) Add the wine and cook for about 2 minutes more, until the pan is dry. Stir in the pepper.

Spoon the mushrooms over the broccolini, then scatter some Parmesan over the top. Serve warm or at room temperature.

VARIATION You can substitute broccoli for the broccolini. Cut the whole broccoli head—crown and stalk—into long spears.

Brassica Sprouts Salad *with* Avocado-Lime Cream

SERVES 4

1 large ripe avocado, halved and pitted

3 tablespoons freshly squeezed lime juice, plus more if needed

3 tablespoons water, plus more if needed

¼ cup fresh basil leaves

1 to 3 teaspoons sliced jalapeño chile (optional)

1 clove garlic, smashed

¾ teaspoon kosher salt (divided)

½ teaspoon freshly ground black pepper (divided)

2 tablespoons olive oil

1 cucumber, halved lengthwise, seeded, patted dry, and thinly sliced

2 carrots, peeled and shaved lengthwise into ribbons with a vegetable peeler

2 cups halved cherry tomatoes

1 to 2 loosely packed cups (or more) brassica sprouts (such as broccoli, radish, or mizuna, or a combination) (see recipe)

BRASSICA SPROUTS USUALLY find their way to the table in minute quantities, most often as a garnish or maybe part of a wrap. The sprouts contain extraordinary health benefits (see The Amazing Brassica Sprout, page 95), however, so I wanted to showcase them in at least one recipe. They can be difficult to find; look for them in natural foods stores and Asian markets. Broccoli and radish sprouts are the most common types—you may also see them labeled "microgreens"—but if you are fortunate to hit the jackpot, you'll find mizuna, kohlrabi, or tatsoi sprouts, as well. A bright blender dressing made from avocado, basil, and lime juice acts as the perfect counterpoint to the peppy sprouts. You can cut the vegetables and make the dressing hours ahead of time, but toss them together just before serving.

Scoop the avocado flesh from its skin into a blender or food processor. Add the lime juice, water, basil, chile, garlic, $1/2$ teaspoon of the salt, and $1/4$ teaspoon of the pepper and puree until smooth. Add the oil and blend to combine. The dressing should be thick. If it seems too thick, add more water or lime juice, 1 tablespoon at a time, until thinned to a workable consistency.

In a large serving bowl, combine the cucumber, carrots, and cherry tomatoes. Just before serving, toss the vegetables with about half of the dressing and the remaining $1/4$ teaspoon each salt and pepper. Taste the salad and add more dressing if needed. (Use any leftover dressing as a dip or to dress another salad. It will keep, covered, in the refrigerator for up to 2 days.) Taste again and add additional salt, pepper, or lime juice if needed. Top the salad with the sprouts and serve immediately.

Homegrown Brassica Sprouts

THERE ARE two issues with purchasing brassica sprouts. The first, as already noted in the brassica sprouts salad recipe, is availability. The second is cost. One good solution is to grow them yourself, though you will need to be patient. One package of seeds takes about a week to grow into 1¹/₂ cups of sprouts. Give this method a try and see if you catch the sprouting bug. If you do, you can purchase special sprouting trays, which will allow you to grow the sprouts in bulk.

Brassica sprouts pack a lot of flavor—in other words, a little goes a long way—and can be a healthful addition to any meal. Stir them into softly scrambled eggs, cooked rice, or quinoa; toss them into salads; or add them to a sandwich or wrap. Or, garnish soups or noodle dishes—Asian dishes seasoned with soy sauce work especially well—with a handful of sprouts.

1 packet organic broccoli, radish, or other brassica seeds

Potting soil

In a small bowl, soak the seeds in water to cover for about 6 hours. Drain off the water. Spread potting soil to a depth of 3 to 4 inches in a shallow pot with good drainage. (Or, you can use seed-sprouting trays.) Sprinkle the seeds on top of the soil fairly densely, distributing about 15 seeds per square inch. Cover the seeds with about a ¹/₈-inch-thick layer of potting soil. Some seeds may still peek through the soil.

Place the pot near a warm, sunny window. Keep the seeds and soil moist by misting them with a spray bottle twice a day. (Misting keeps the seeds moist without washing them together in a big flood of water.) After 3 days, the seeds should start to sprout. When the sprouts are about 4 inches tall (after about 7 or 8 days), they are ready to harvest. Use scissors to clip the sprouts close to the base. Rinse before using.

Broccoli

watercress

cress

*mustard
greens*

CHAPTER FIVE

Leafy Brassicas

Collard Greens, Mustard Greens, Broccoli Rabe,
Arugula, and Cress

broccoli rabe　　　　　*collard greens*　　　　　*arugula*

The leafy brassicas, unlike, say, a dainty head of butter lettuce, declare their distinctive personalities up front. They lack for nothing in the flavor department, showcasing a range from mildly bittersweet to aggressively hot and spicy. These nutritional giants offer not only the cancer-preventing properties of other brassicas but also the benefits of high calcium, iron, and fiber found in many dark, leafy greens.

Collard Greens

Collards are full flavored and sweet, with a mild bitterness. The flat paddlelike leaves feel thick and almost leathery and retain a pleasant chewiness when cooked. Smaller leaves are predictably more tender.

SELECTION Collard greens are sold in bunches, ranging from 8 ounces to about 1 pound. Choose fresh-looking greens, bright green to olive; avoid bunches with wilted, slimy, or yellowed leaves.

PREP Remove rubber bands or twist ties from the collards and put the leaves, along with a paper towel to wick away extra moisture, in a loosely sealed plastic bag. Refrigerate for up to 3 or 4 days. When ready to use, wash the greens (see page 7) and remove the tough center ribs (see V Cut on page 8) and the stems, as they are unpleasant to chew. Dry the greens well. To cut collard greens, stack the leaves and roll them up lengthwise into a tight cigar shape, then cut crosswise as instructed in individual recipes. Collard greens take well to either a quick sauté or a long braise, their flavor mellowing in the heat. Only the youngest, most tender collards should be served raw.

NUTRITION Collards are a great source of calcium, iron, fiber, potassium, folate, and vitamins C, K, and A. They contain about 11 calories per cup.

Mustard Greens

Although there are many types of mustard greens of varying levels of flavor intensity, most of them taste sharp, strong, and pungent. (Think of the heat from prepared mustard or mustard oil, which derives from the same plant.) Mustard's spicy bite can be tamed by cooking, or by pairing the greens with a mellow, starchy partner like pasta or beans.

SELECTION Sold in bunches that weigh from 8 to 12 ounces, mustard greens vary in color and appearance from smooth, red or purple leaves to the frilly, lime green variety most often found in grocery stores. Choose fresh-looking greens; avoid bunches with limp, yellowed, or damp leaves.

PREP Remove rubber bands or twist ties from bunches and put the leaves, along with a paper towel to absorb excess moisture, in a loosely sealed plastic bag. Mustard greens are sturdy but tender and perishable; refrigerate them for no more than 3 days. When ready to use, wash the leaves (see page 7) and remove the tough center ribs (see V Cut on page 8) and the stems if needed. (The center rib of mustard greens can vary: some are slim and tender and others are thick and inedible.) Dry the greens well. To cut mustard greens, stack the leaves and roll them up lengthwise into a tight cigar shape, then cut the leaves crosswise as instructed in individual recipes. Only very tiny young mustard leaves should be eaten raw in salads.

NUTRITION Mustard greens are high in vitamins A, K, and C and in calcium, fiber, and potassium. They contain about 15 calories per cup.

Broccoli Rabe (also known as broccoli raab and rapini)

Don't think of broccoli rabe as a substitute for broccoli. Think of it as a bitter green instead. Its flavor is assertive, bold, and slightly grassy, often finishing with bitterness or pungency, depending on the crop. The stalks, leaves, and florets are all edible. Springtime harvests are leafier and often have a milder flavor.

SELECTION Choose bright green bunches with thin, firm stalks and tight florets, the leafier the better. Bunches generally weigh about 1 to 1¹/₂ pounds.

PREP Remove rubber bands or twist ties from bunches, pop them into a loosely sealed plastic bag, add a paper towel to wick away excess moisture, and refrigerate for no more than 3 or 4 days. When ready to use, trim off about 1/2 inch from the end of each stalk, or trim more if the stalks are stringy or split. Rinse the broccoli rabe well and cut into smaller pieces before cooking. If you find broccoli rabe too assertive for your palate, give it a quick blanch to tame its bite. Be sure to remove excess moisture—you may actually need to wring it out—before sautéing it or your dish will taste watery. Sample the broccoli rabe as you cook it; the stalks can turn from perfectly done to stringy rather quickly. Raw broccoli rabe is not particularly enjoyable.

NUTRITION Enjoy broccoli rabe as a good source for vitamins A, C, and K, plus iron, calcium, potassium, and folic acid. It has about 9 calories per cup.

Arugula (also known as rocket) and Cress (watercress, upland cress)

Arugula and cress, most often used in salads, taste bold and peppery, sometimes spicy. If you find the leaves too assertively flavored, mix them with milder greens for a balanced salad. These greens take well to wilting, needing only a quick toss with something hot—cooked pasta, for instance—to soften their bite. They also make a brilliant bed for grilled meats, wilting slightly as they absorb the savory meat juices.

SELECTION Arugula is sold in small bunches or as prewashed "baby" arugula, either packaged or in bulk. The long, slender leaves are sword shaped and deeply notched. Watercress, which is grown in water (either cultivated or wild) and has small, rich green, rounded leaves and thick stems, is marketed in bunches, as well. Upland cress, also known as land cress, has round, green leaves and light, wispy edible stems. It is often sold with the roots surrounded by a ball of dirt still attached. You will likely find only one type of cress at the store; use them interchangeably. Choose arugula or cress with bright green leaves; pass up bunches or bags with wilted, yellowed, or overly wet leaves.

PREP Remove rubber bands or twist ties from arugula or cress, put the leaves in a loosely sealed plastic bag, and slip in a paper towel to absorb excess moisture. These greens are highly perishable, so refrigerate for no more than 2 days. When ready to use, wash the greens well (see page 7)—arugula is generally quite dirty—and remove any thick or tough stems. Dry the greens well, especially if they are headed to a salad bowl. Enjoy them raw or lightly wilted.

NUTRITION Both greens are high in cancer-preventing glucosinolates as well as vitamins A and C, calcium, iron, and folic acid. They contain about 4 calories per cup.

The Amazing Brassica Sprout

BY ANDREA NAKAYAMA

Take a seed, any seed. As it begins to sprout, there is an activation of energy and the germination of a new life. You witness that fresh life emerge in the form of a sweet green tail that grows and twists into a crunchy and delightful morsel that tickles both your tongue and your taste buds.

If we focus down to the microscopic level—perhaps through the eyes of an ant witnessing this inaugural growth—we can see that as a seed begins to sprout, catalysts are being produced within the kernel. Those catalysts, otherwise known as enzymes, serve to convert the dense and compact nutrients within the seed into a flourishing plant. Right inside that first tiny shoot you will find vitamins, minerals, amino acids, essential fats, and complex carbohydrates. These are all the things that *we* need to grow and thrive.

The health benefits of a sprout depend on the seed from which it began. Overall, sprouts are both an efficient and delicious way to increase easy-to-assimilate nutrients in your diet. They carry the same nutritional profile as their full-grown counterparts. Yet a broccoli sprout contains those nutrients in a far more concentrated measure than a head of broccoli. Sprouts may seem small and insignificant, a sprinkling atop your salad, in your sandwich, or on your stir-fry, but they are the powerhouse of the plant kingdom.

When used in abundance, brassica sprouts have the unique ability to support keeping your body young and healthy. They help to increase your immune response, warding off colds and flus and even certain types of cancer. Sprouts contain fiber that assists in helping you to detoxify and maintain good colon health. And because sprouts are *alive* and growing until the moment we eat them, I believe that they also bring a taste of enthusiasm for life itself—that is, they awaken our vitality. After all, we are what we eat and what our body can do with what we eat!

Brassica sprouts are grown from the seeds of broccoli, broccoli rabe, cabbage, cauliflower, kale, collards, turnip, rutabaga, kohlrabi, Brussels sprouts, mustard greens, and Asian greens like bok choy. They are potent sources of the B vitamins, which I like to call our antistress vitamins; vitamin E, which helps to protect the heart and keep us fertile; and vitamin C, a beautiful vitamin for our skin, teeth, and immunity.

ANDREA NAKAYAMA *is a nutritionist at* replenish pdx *who applies her passion for healing to studying and teaching the science behind nutrition and physiology.*

Though I do not believe that a plant will spring up where no seed has been, I have great faith in a seed. Convince me that you have a seed there, and I am prepared to expect wonders.

—HENRY DAVID THOREAU

Quick Collards Sauté

SERVES 4 TO 6

1½ pounds collard greens (about 2 bunches), center ribs and tough stems removed

3 tablespoons olive oil

4 cloves garlic, minced

¼ teaspoon red pepper flakes

½ teaspoon kosher salt

YOU ARE PROBABLY MOST FAMILIAR with the slow-cooked collards of the South, a treatment that yields delicious greens but fails to celebrate their inherent brightness. When it comes to cooking collards, I like to follow the Brazilian tradition that calls for a quick sauté. Shred the leaves as thinly as you can and they will cook in no time. I like to serve a mound of these collards topped with an over-easy egg for breakfast. Break the yolk and let it ooze throughout the greens as a tasty sauce.

Stack the collard leaves, roll them up lengthwise into a tight cigar shape, and, using a chef's knife, cut the greens crosswise into very thin shreds. Rinse them well and spin them dry. (You can rinse the greens before or after shredding; I prefer to rinse them after.)

Unless you have an extremely large pan, plan to cook the collards in two batches. They will cook down significantly, though not as much as spinach. Heat half of the oil in a large (12 inches or wider), deep frying pan over medium heat. Add half of the garlic and cook, stirring, for about 30 seconds, until fragrant. Add half of the collards and turn them with tongs to coat them with the garlicky oil. (You may need to add the greens in batches and let the first batch wilt before adding more.) Stir in half of the red pepper flakes and ¼ teaspoon of the salt. Cook the greens, turning them occasionally, for 3 to 4 minutes, until wilted. Transfer the collards to a serving bowl and repeat with the remaining oil, garlic, greens, red pepper flakes, and salt. Serve hot or at room temperature.

VARIATIONS This sauté works equally well with other greens, such as kale or kohlrabi greens. If you prefer softer greens, add a few minutes to the cooking time or cover the pan and steam them off the heat for 5 minutes.

Curried Collard Greens

SERVES 4

2 tablespoons unsalted butter

1 yellow onion, thinly sliced

1 jalapeño chile (or less if you prefer), stemmed, seeded, and thinly sliced

1½ teaspoons ground cumin

1 teaspoon ground coriander

½ teaspoon ground turmeric

2 bunches collard greens (about 1½ pounds total), center ribs and tough stems removed, leaves cut crosswise into narrow ribbons

¾ teaspoon kosher salt

6 tablespoons water

2 teaspoons freshly squeezed lemon juice

COLLARD GREENS HAVE YET to catch on in American kitchens, but globally the greens receive royal treatment. Here, I am sharing a quick-braised dish based on two of my favorite recipes made with the greens, Ethiopian *gomen wat* and Indian *saag*. I concocted a hybrid version, sautéing the greens in butter, onions, fresh chile, and spices and then letting the flavors blend for a few minutes under cover. Taste a little of the chile before you add the slices to the pan, as some jalapeños are very spicy and some are almost as mild as bell peppers, and you may want to adjust the amount called for here. Because the greens have a complex flavor, you can serve them alongside simply seasoned grilled chicken thighs, lamb, or pork chops.

In a medium pot, melt the butter over medium heat. Add the onion and chile and cook, stirring occasionally, for about 5 minutes, until the onion starts to soften. Stir in the cumin, coriander, and turmeric.

Add the collard greens and turn them with tongs to coat them with the spiced onion. (You may need to add the greens in batches and let the first batch wilt before adding more.) Stir in the salt and water, turn down the heat to medium-low, cover, and cook, stirring occasionally, for about 15 minutes, until the greens are wilted and tender. If you prefer softer greens, remove the pan from the heat and steam the greens, covered, for 5 minutes longer. Stir in the lemon juice and serve hot or at room temperature.

VARIATION For a vegan or dairy-free version, substitute canola or another neutral oil for the butter.

WHENEVER I PICK UP collard wraps from a juice bar or a vegan restaurant, I notice the collards are often raw. You can use raw greens, assuming you can find bunches of small, tender leaves, but I steam the leaves for a minute just to take the raw edge off and make them easier to roll. (Take a bite of a raw leaf; you will know right away whether you want to chew through a whole one or not.) Spread a dollop of store-bought peanut sauce on each leaf—you can use homemade peanut- or almond-butter sauce if you prefer—and then stack slices of mango, avocado, and bell pepper on top. Roll up each leaf into a cone and set the cones on a platter for lunch, an after-school snack, or a unique appetizer. If you refrigerate the wraps before serving, squeeze a bit of lime juice over the avocado to keep it from browning.

Sunshine Wraps

MAKES 8 TO 10 WRAPS

1 bunch small collard greens (8 to 10 leaves)

½ cup store-bought Asian peanut sauce

8 to 10 or more thinly sliced mango or papaya spears (at least 1 slice per wrap)

1 ripe avocado, halved, pitted, peeled, thinly sliced lengthwise, and slices sprinkled with a large pinch of kosher salt (at least 1 slice per wrap)

1 red bell pepper, cut lengthwise into narrow strips

Cut off the collard stems at the point where they meet the leaves. Using a paring knife, shave down the center rib until it is almost even with the leaf. (Don't cut the stem out, as it will leave a hole.) Set up a collapsible steamer basket in a large pot over (not touching) an inch or two of water and bring the water to a boil. Put the leaves in the basket, cover the pot, and steam for 30 to 60 seconds, just until wilted. Lay the collard leaves in a single layer on a clean kitchen towel to dry. Pat them dry before using.

Line up the steamed leaves, with the base of each leaf nearest you and the shaved stem side down, on a countertop or cutting board. Spread a teaspoon or two of the peanut sauce in the center of each leaf. Center a mango spear, an avocado slice, and a few bell pepper strips lengthwise near the top of each leaf, extending them just beyond the edge. You want the filling to "peek" out the top of each wrap.

If this is your first time rolling collard wraps, start with the largest leaves, which are easier to roll. First, fold the bottom left side of each leaf toward the center of the right side, forming one side of the cone. Fold the bottom of each leaf up to the center and then roll the leaf from left to right into a cone shape. As the wraps are formed, put them, seam side down, on a plate. Serve immediately or cover and refrigerate for up to 2 hours. Serve chilled or at room temperature.

VARIATIONS Wrap other vegetables, such as shredded raw zucchini, carrots, or red cabbage, in the leaves. You can tuck some cooked protein, such as sliced chicken or white fish or whole or halved shrimp, into each wrap, too.

Spanish Tortilla *with* Mustard Greens

SERVES 4

3 tablespoons olive oil

1 small yellow onion, sliced

1 large baking potato (about 1 pound), peeled and cut into ½-inch dice

1¼ teaspoons kosher salt (divided)

1 small bunch mustard greens, large stems removed, center ribs removed if desired, leaves coarsely chopped (4 to 6 cups)

8 eggs

¼ teaspoon freshly ground black pepper

UNLIKE THE THIN CORN or flour tortillas used in Mexican cooking, a Spanish tortilla more closely resembles a frittata. Traditionally, sliced potatoes and onions are poached in a generous amount of olive oil and then meet up with beaten eggs to form a thick, sliceable omelet. My version uses diced potato and significantly less oil without sacrificing flavor. Once the onion and potato are cooked, start adding the mustard greens to the pan a little at a time, allowing each batch to wilt a bit before adding more. If the pan gets too full, you have added enough, but you should be able to accommodate at least 4 cups of chopped greens. Spanish recipes often instruct you to invert the tortilla onto a plate and slide it back in the pan to finish the cooking, but I think popping it under the broiler for a few minutes is a much easier method for home cooks.

This tortilla tastes delicious with the *romesco* sauce from Broccoli Rabe with Romesco Sauce (page 104). The sauce will keep in the refrigerator for up to 4 days, so consider saving any leftover sauce—or making extra—to serve with this dish.

Heat the oil in a 10- to 12-inch nonstick frying pan over medium heat. Add the onion, potato, and ³/₄ teaspoon of the salt and cook, stirring frequently, for 10 to 15 minutes, until the potato is cooked. (Taste a piece of potato to check for doneness.) Stir in the mustard greens, a handful at a time, until they all fit in the pan. Cook for about 3 minutes, until the greens are wilted.

Preheat the broiler. In a bowl, beat the eggs until blended. Stir the remaining ¹/₂ teaspoon salt and the pepper into the eggs. With the pan still over medium heat, spread the vegetables evenly over the bottom and pour the eggs over the vegetables. Cook for about 3 minutes, until the eggs are set around the edges. Transfer the pan to the broiler about 3 inches from the heat source. (If the handle is not ovenproof, wrap it in a few layers of aluminum foil.) Broil the tortilla for 2 to 3 minutes, until the eggs are set and the top is browned. A knife inserted into the tortilla should come out clean.

Slide the tortilla onto a cutting board or a serving plate. Cut into wedges and serve warm or at room temperature.

MUSTARD GREENS CAN HAVE a sharp bite, but I find that a pile of rich, nearly melted caramelized onions acts as a calming companion. The onions add a surprising sweetness to the greens, one that you can leave as is or temper with sherry vinegar. Collard greens have a bulky center rib that always needs removal, but mustard greens often have softer stems. Cut off the larger stems and cut out or leave the center rib according to your preference. The greens will cook down quite a bit (though not as much as spinach), but you'll still need to choose a pan large enough to accommodate them. Just add a few handfuls of the greens at a time until they all wilt in the pan.

Heat the oil in a large (12 inches or wider), deep frying pan over medium heat. Add the onion and 1/4 teaspoon of the salt and cook, stirring frequently, for about 20 minutes, until the onions are golden brown and caramelized. If the onion is browning too quickly, turn down the heat to medium-low; you want the onion to be golden and soft, not crisp.

Add the mustard greens—a handful at a time until they all fit in the pan—and turn them with tongs to combine them with the onions. Stir in the remaining 1/4 teaspoon salt and the pepper. Cook, turning the greens as needed, for about 5 minutes, until they are tender and wilted. If the pan seems too dry as you are cooking, add 1 tablespoon water to the greens. If you prefer softer greens, remove the pan from the heat, cover, and steam for a few more minutes. Taste the greens. If the onion added too much sweetness, add more pepper or the vinegar to balance the flavors. Serve hot or at room temperature.

VARIATIONS Substitute kale or collard greens for the mustard greens. For a little spicy heat, add a pinch of red pepper flakes with the greens. Bacon is a good addition, too. Before you add the onion, fry a few slices of bacon in the pan until they render their fat and are cooked, then transfer them to paper towels to drain. Cook the onion in the rendered bacon fat in place of the oil. Chop the bacon and stir it into the greens just before serving.

Mustard Greens *with* Caramelized Sweet Onion

SERVES 4

3 tablespoons olive oil

1 large sweet onion (such as Walla Walla or Vidalia), thinly sliced

1/2 teaspoon kosher salt (divided)

2 bunches mustard greens (about 1 pound total), large stems removed, center ribs removed if desired, leaves stacked, and shredded crosswise

1/4 teaspoon freshly ground black pepper

Splash of sherry vinegar (optional)

Clyde Common's Broccoli Rabe Salad *with* Pistachios *and* Lemon Vinaigrette

SERVES 6

CHEF CHRIS DIMINNO of Clyde Common restaurant in Portland, Oregon, makes an amazing lemony broccoli rabe salad. I knew the flavor had to come from something other than simply lemon juice, and that "secret ingredient" turns out to be lemon oil. The oil is simple to make—just infuse lemon zest in a blend of oils (olive oil alone tastes too bitter) for 12 hours—but you need to plan ahead. (If you are pressed for time, purchase a high-quality lemon oil and use 1 cup of it.) I tried to stay true to chef DiMinno's original salad recipe, changing only the quantity of the dressing (I halved it) and using white wine vinegar instead of a combination of white wine vinegar and late-harvest Sauvignon Blanc vinegar. The recipe still makes more dressing than you will need—it is hard to call for less than one egg yolk—but it is so good that I guarantee it will not go to waste. Serve the extra dressing over asparagus, broccoli, green beans, grilled romaine, or any simple salad.

Since this is a restaurant dish, the process is slightly more involved than many of the other recipes here, but it is also very special. Showcase it topped with eggs sunny-side up, or serve it alongside a simple protein—grilled salmon, perhaps—for dinner guests. At Clyde Common, the broccoli rabe is served in whole stalks (knife-and-fork style), but I like to cut the stalks into about 2-inch lengths. You can do it either way.

To make the lemon oil, combine the olive oil, neutral oil, and lemon zest in a large measuring cup. Cover and let stand at room temperature for about 12 hours. Strain the oil through a fine-mesh sieve into a clean container and discard the zest. Cover and store at room temperature; it will keep for up to 2 days. Alternatively, strain the oil directly into the blender as you are making the dressing.

To make the dressing, in a blender, combine the lemon juice, egg yolk, vinegar, honey, mustard, and 1/4 teaspoon each of the salt and pepper. Cover the blender, turn it on to medium speed, and slowly drizzle the lemon oil through the opening in the lid to form an emulsified dressing. The dressing should be thick but pourable. If the dressing is too thick, stir in a little room-temperature water as needed to thin it. (The dressing can be prepared up to 2 days ahead. Store in an airtight container in the refrigerator until ready to use.)

Set up a collapsible steamer basket in a large pot over (not touching) an inch or two of water and bring the water to a boil. Put the broccoli rabe in the basket, cover the pot, and steam for 2 to 3 minutes, until bright green and tender; the timing will depend on the thickness of the stems. You may need to do this in two batches. (Broccoli rabe overcooks quickly; remove it from the heat when it seems just done or the stalks will get stringy.) Remove the broccoli rabe and set it on a wire rack or a clean kitchen towel to cool. Pat dry if needed.

In a large bowl, combine the broccoli rabe, pistachios, and herbs. Add half of the dressing and the remaining 1/4 teaspoon each salt and pepper and, using tongs, toss to combine. Taste and add additional dressing, salt, or pepper if needed. Serve the salad on a platter or on individual plates and top with the cured meats. For a light main course, top each serving with an egg.

VARIATIONS Substitute broccolini for the broccoli rabe. For a vegetarian version, omit the cured meat.

½ cup olive oil

½ cup neutral-flavored oil (such as canola or grapeseed)

Grated zest of 5 lemons

2 tablespoons freshly squeezed lemon juice

1 egg yolk

1½ tablespoons white wine vinegar

1½ teaspoons honey

¾ teaspoon Dijon mustard

½ teaspoon kosher salt (divided)

½ teaspoon freshly ground black pepper (divided)

2 bunches broccoli rabe (about 2 pounds total), ends trimmed and discarded, remaining stalks and leaves cut into 2-inch lengths

½ cup shelled unsalted pistachios, coarsely chopped

½ cup mixed fresh herbs (preferably flat-leaf parsley leaves, tarragon leaves, and snipped chives)

2 ounces sliced cured meat (such as salami, soppressata, or prosciutto), cut into narrow strips (optional)

6 eggs, cooked sunny-side up, for serving (optional)

Broccoli Rabe *with* Romesco Sauce

SERVES 4

½ cup slivered almonds, toasted (see page 13)

2 cloves garlic

¼ teaspoon sweet Spanish smoked paprika (pimentón de la Vera)

¼ teaspoon cayenne pepper, or more for a spicier sauce

1 cup roasted red bell pepper strips (jarred is fine; pat them dry)

1 plum tomato, seeded and coarsely chopped

2 teaspoons red wine vinegar

3 tablespoons olive oil

¾ teaspoon kosher salt

¼ teaspoon freshly ground black pepper

1 bunch broccoli rabe (about 1 pound), ends trimmed and discarded, remaining stalks and leaves cut into 2-inch lengths

HERE, I HAVE PAIRED bold-flavored broccoli rabe with an equally robust Spanish-inspired *romesco* sauce. The recipe makes plenty of *romesco*, at least enough to sauce a couple bunches of broccoli rabe if you are cooking for a crowd. But I doubt that extra *romesco* will be a concern; my family spoons it over just about everything: steak, salmon, potatoes, corn on the cob. If you do have leftover sauce, try it on the Spanish Tortilla with Mustard Greens (page 100). *Pimentón de la Vera*, a specialty of Extremadura, in western Spain, is a smoked paprika made from locally grown small peppers that are dried over an oak-wood fire and then finely ground. Both sweet and hot versions are available. You can find the paprika in the spices aisle of many grocery stores. If broccoli rabe is hard to find (or out of season), try one of the variations.

To make the *romesco* sauce, in a food processor, combine the almonds, garlic, smoked paprika, and cayenne pepper and pulse until coarsely chopped. Add the roasted pepper, tomato, and vinegar. With the machine running, add the oil in a thin stream through the feed tube and process until a coarse puree forms. Season with the salt and black pepper. Taste and add more salt or pepper if needed. (The sauce can be made up to 4 days in advance and stored in an airtight container in the refrigerator.)

Set up a collapsible steamer basket in a large pot over (not touching) an inch or two of water and bring the water to a boil. Put the broccoli rabe in the basket, cover the pot, and steam for 2 to 3 minutes, until bright green and tender; the timing will depend on the thickness of the stems. (Broccoli rabe overcooks quickly; remove it from the heat when it seems just done or the stalks will get stringy.) If the broccoli rabe is very wet, put it on a clean kitchen towel and pat it dry.

Put the broccoli rabe on a serving platter and drizzle some of the sauce over the top. Alternatively, toss the broccoli rabe with some of the sauce to coat it evenly. Pass the remaining sauce at the table. Serve warm or at room temperature.

VARIATION *Romesco* sauce pairs well with many brassicas. Try it with roasted Brussels sprouts, cauliflower, broccoli, or broccolini.

YOU MAY NOTICE some visual similarities between the green buds near the top of a bunch of broccoli rabe and the florets on regular broccoli, but the resemblance ends there. Broccoli rabe packs an assertive, yet addictive punch that tastes nothing like broccoli. Trim off the ends of the stalks, and the remainder—leaves, thin stalks, florets—is entirely edible. I've found that the most successful way to cook broccoli rabe is either to sauté it quickly or steam it. Many cooks blanch broccoli rabe in boiling water for a minute or two to reduce the bitterness. Although this works, it leaves the vegetables so waterlogged that you need to wring them out before you can sauté them. I consider the bitterness an asset and pair it with equally bold flavors that can stare it down.

Use this as a basic side dish, or try one of my favorite meals—pasta with sausage and broccoli rabe. Sauté about 8 ounces Italian fennel or other sausage, either bulk or removed from its casing, in the frying pan until cooked through, then transfer to a bowl. Sauté the broccoli rabe in the same pan as directed and stir in the sausage at the end. Toss the mixture with cooked pasta, extra olive oil, and grated Parmesan cheese. The broccoli rabe is also delicious stirred into cooked white beans or soft polenta, or layered with sliced roast pork and provolone cheese in warm *panini*.

Classic Sautéed Broccoli Rabe *with* Garlic *and* Anchovies

SERVES 4

2 tablespoons olive oil, plus more for drizzling

3 cloves garlic, minced

4 oil-packed anchovy fillets, minced (don't worry about any tiny bones; they are soft and edible)

1 large bunch broccoli rabe (about 1¼ pounds), ends trimmed and discarded, remaining stalks and leaves cut crosswise into 2-inch lengths

¼ teaspoon kosher salt

Heat the oil, garlic, and anchovies in a large (12 inches or wider), deep frying pan over medium heat. When the garlic starts to sizzle, add the broccoli rabe and the salt. Turn the greens with tongs to coat them with the flavored oil. Cook, turning the greens occasionally, for about 3 minutes or more, until just tender; the timing will depend on the thickness of the stalks. If the stalks are especially thick, add 1 or 2 tablespoons water, cover the pan, and cook for 2 minutes more. Watch closely, however, as the stalks can go from tender to stringy in a heartbeat. Serve hot or at room temperature, drizzled with a bit of olive oil.

Watercress Salad *with* Ginger Carrot Dressing

SERVES 4

2 tablespoons peeled, chopped fresh ginger

2 green onions, whites and green parts, coarsely chopped

1 carrot, peeled and cut into chunks

3 tablespoons freshly squeezed lemon juice

2 tablespoons soy sauce or tamari

1 tablespoon toasted sesame oil

1 tablespoon water

½ teaspoon kosher salt (divided)

½ teaspoon freshly ground black pepper (divided)

3 tablespoons canola or other neutral oil

2 bunches watercress or upland cress, thick stems removed (10 to 12 cups loosely packed)

1 bunch radishes, trimmed and thinly sliced

WHEN SEARCHING FOR CRESS, you may come upon bundles of wiry watercress roped together with a rubber band, or wispy land cress with a ball of dirt attached to the roots. Since you never know what you are going to find, it's hard to guess what a standard "bunch" weighs. Aim for 10 or 12 cups of loosely packed greens for a salad for four, which equates to about 2 small bunches. If you do not have cress, try baby arugula, baby spinach, mixed greens, or a combination. The gingery carrot dressing may remind you of one you have tasted in a Japanese restaurant. Since the dressing is so delectable, the recipe yields a generous amount. You will need only about half of it for the salad. Save the remainder for another salad, for drizzling over a simple main dish like grilled salmon, shrimp, or pork, or for spooning over rice.

In a food processor, combine the ginger, green onions, and carrot and pulse several times to chop finely. Scrape down the bowl with a spatula, then add the lemon juice, soy sauce, sesame oil, water, and ¼ teaspoon each of the salt and pepper. With the machine running, add the canola oil in a steady stream through the feed tube to form an emulsified dressing.

Put the watercress and radishes in a serving bowl. Drizzle with half of the dressing, add the remaining ¼ teaspoon each salt and pepper, and toss to coat evenly. Taste and add more dressing if needed. (Store the remaining dressing in an airtight container in the refrigerator for up to 2 days.) Serve immediately.

VARIATIONS Instead of cress, use baby arugula or mizuna (both brassicas) or mixed salad greens. Add halved cherry tomatoes, diced avocado, or carrot ribbons to the salad, or sprinkle toasted sesame seeds over the top.

SERVING AN ARUGULA SALAD with fruit and goat cheese is a cliché, but like most clichés, there's a good reason for it. The combination works. The sweetness of the fruit plus the creaminess of the cheese balance the peppery bite of greens like arugula or cress. I often combine both kinds of greens in this salad, but you could choose one or even combine them with something less assertive, like baby spinach. I also sometimes purchase 5-ounce packages of prewashed baby arugula for this salad. Large bundles of arugula are often so sandy that washing the leaves makes them irretrievably wilted. I save the bundled arugula for hot dishes in which the leaves will be wilted anyway.

Change the fruit depending on the season, using ripe peaches in summer, pears or figs (even dried figs rehydrated in a bit of water) in fall, and persimmons in winter. Add nuts or pumpkin seeds if you like a little crunch, or strips of *serrano* ham or prosciutto for a salty twist.

Peppery Greens Salad

SERVES 4

5 ounces arugula and/or cress leaves (about 12 cups loosely packed)

¾ cup diced soft fruit (such as peaches, nectarines, figs, or pears)

¼ teaspoon kosher salt

¼ teaspoon freshly ground black pepper

2 tablespoons olive oil

1½ tablespoons balsamic vinegar

½ cup crumbled soft goat cheese (about 2 ounces)

Put the greens and fruit in a serving bowl. Sprinkle with the salt and pepper, drizzle with the oil and vinegar, and toss to coat evenly. (If you are not using the full amount of greens, make the vinaigrette in a small bowl, whisking together the salt, pepper, and vinegar, then whisking in the oil. Add as much of the vinaigrette as needed to dress the salad lightly, being careful not to overdress it.) Add the goat cheese and toss gently to incorporate. Taste and add more salt and pepper if needed. Serve immediately.

VARIATION For a crisper, less sweet salad, combine the greens with 1 apple, thinly sliced; 1 fennel bulb, thinly sliced, and a dressing made from 1 1/2 tablespoons freshly squeezed lemon juice, 1 teaspoon honey, and 2 tablespoons olive oil. Season to taste with kosher salt and freshly ground black pepper.

SOBA NOODLES, hearty and flavorful Japanese noodles made from either buckwheat only or buckwheat and wheat flour, pair perfectly with peppery watercress and a spicy dressing. This hassle-free side dish could not be easier, requiring no cutting at all. The watercress does not need cooking; it just needs a quick wilt, so tossing it in the hot pan with the freshly cooked noodles and sauce will do the trick. Look for the soba noodles, chile-garlic sauce (a mixture of chile, garlic, and vinegar), and toasted sesame oil in the Asian foods section of your grocery store. If you find watercress, a large bunch should be enough. If only upland cress is available, grab a couple small bunches.

Spicy Soba Noodles *with* Wilted Watercress

SERVES 4

8 ounces dried soba noodles

2½ tablespoons soy sauce or tamari

1 teaspoon chile-garlic sauce

1 teaspoon toasted sesame oil

6 cups stemmed watercress or upland cress

1 tablespoon canola or other neutral oil

Bring a large pot of water to a boil over high heat. Add the noodles and cook for about 8 minutes, or according to package directions, until done. Meanwhile, to make the sauce, in a small bowl, stir together the soy sauce, chile-garlic sauce, and sesame oil.

Drain the noodles in a colander set in the sink. Put the watercress in the hot pan. (If you are using 100 percent buckwheat soba, the noodles may be excessively starchy. Give them a quick rinse with hot tap water.) Return the noodles to the pan along with the canola oil. Using tongs, toss to combine. The watercress should wilt from the residual heat of the pan and the noodles. Add the sauce and toss until well incorporated. Serve warm or at room temperature.

VARIATION Substitute 6 cups arugula for the cress. Most soba noodles are made from a combination of buckwheat and wheat flour. If you are following a gluten-free diet, you'll need to seek out 100 percent buckwheat soba. Eden and Mitoku are two good brands. You'll also need to use wheat-free tamari or soy sauce.

Leafy Brassicas

White Pizza *with* Arugula *and* Prosciutto

MAKES ONE (10- TO 12-INCH) PIZZA

½ cup ricotta cheese

3 tablespoons grated Parmesan cheese

Kosher salt and freshly ground black pepper

8 ounces pizza dough, at room temperature

2 cups arugula leaves

2 to 3 slices prosciutto, cut into narrow strips (optional)

1 tablespoon olive oil

2 teaspoons freshly squeezed lemon juice

YOU ARE LIKELY MORE FAMILIAR with arugula as a simple salad green than as salad-on-top-of-a-pizza green. Here, the residual heat from the crust and creamy warmth of the ricotta temper the peppery bite of the arugula, which is why pizzas like this one are popular on menus throughout the country. Many grocery stores and pizza parlors sell premade pizza dough, which makes this recipe perfect for weeknight cooking. If you are following a gluten-free diet, look for a gluten-free box mix or frozen crust and follow the package directions. If the crust needs longer than 10 to 12 minutes in the oven, prebake the crust partially, then add the cheese topping for the final 10 minutes.

Place a pizza stone on an oven rack in the top third of the oven and preheat the oven to 500°F for a full 30 minutes. In a small bowl, stir together the ricotta, Parmesan, and ¼ teaspoon each salt and pepper, mixing well.

Lay a sheet of parchment paper 12 to 14 inches square on a work surface. Place the dough on the parchment and roll or pat it into a 10- to 12-inch round about ⅛ inch thick. Using the back of a spoon, spread the cheese mixture evenly over the crust. Transfer the parchment to a rimless or an inverted baking sheet. Slide the pizza—parchment and all—onto the hot baking stone and bake for 10 to 12 minutes, until the crust is crisp and the topping is browned. (If you do not have a baking stone, slide the pizza and parchment onto a rimless baking sheet and bake for 12 to 14 minutes. The crust will not be quite as crisp.)

Just before the pizza is ready to come out of the oven, combine the arugula and prosciutto in a bowl. Drizzle with the oil and lemon juice, add a pinch of salt and a generous grind of pepper, and toss to coat evenly. Remove the pizza from the oven and mound the salad on top. The heat from the pizza will wilt the greens. Serve immediately, cut into wedges.

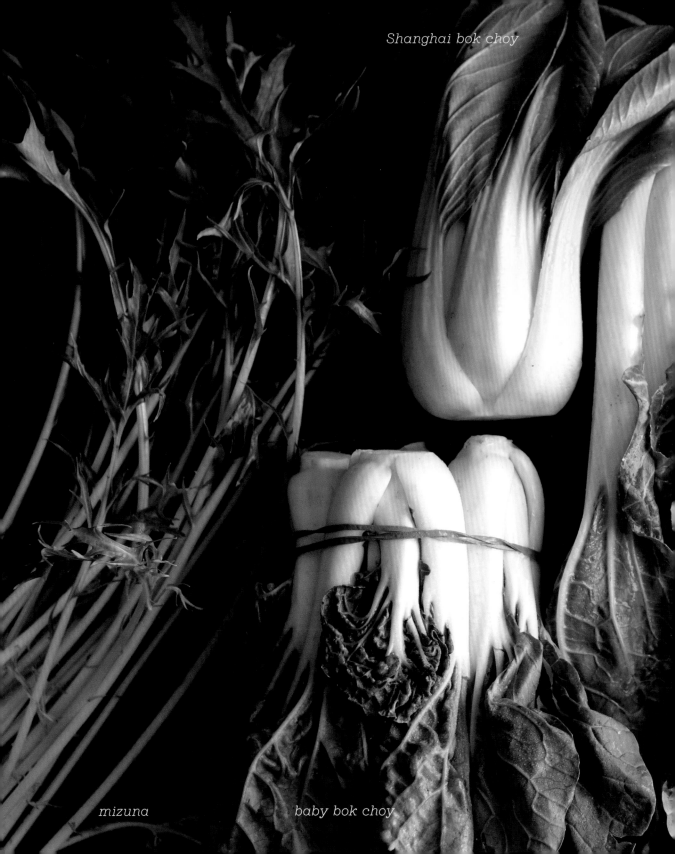

Shanghai bok choy

mizuna

baby bok choy

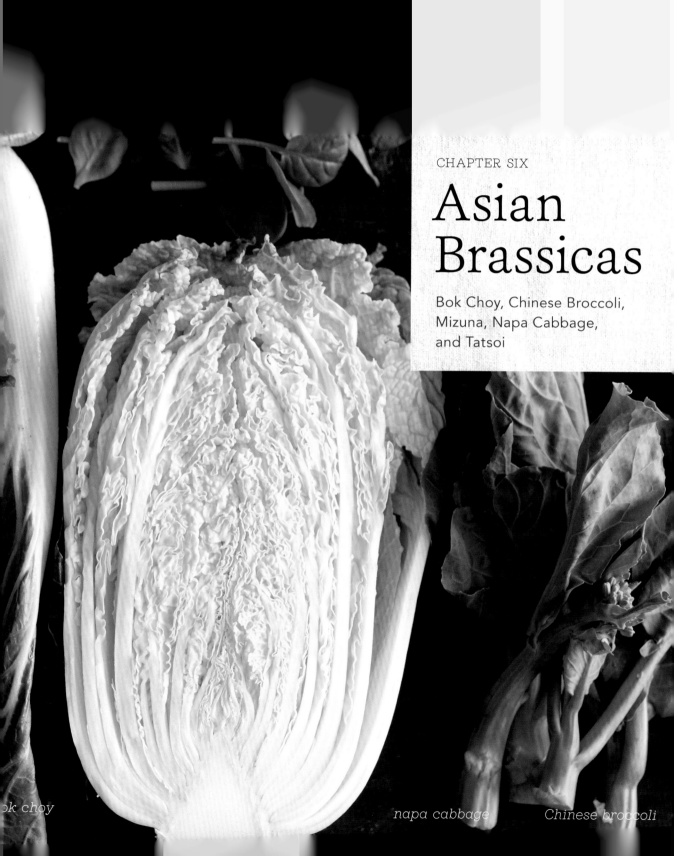

CHAPTER SIX

Asian Brassicas

Bok Choy, Chinese Broccoli,
Mizuna, Napa Cabbage,
and Tatsoi

ok choy

napa cabbage

Chinese broccoli

Make room in your kitchen for the Asian brassicas—bok choy, Chinese broc-coli, mizuna, napa cabbage, tatsoi—and you will find yourself making dozens of tasty, healthful new dishes. While the leafy greens in the previous chap-ter typically have strong flavors, this group boast attributes best described as sweet, juicy, and crisp. Do not limit their use to Asian-inspired recipes, as these greens also make wonderful additions to salads, soups, and side dishes of all kinds. Bok choy and napa cabbage are readily available at grocery stores; Chinese broccoli, mizuna, and tatsoi are harder to find. Look for them at Asian markets, farmers' markets, or natural foods stores, or try the reci-pes using one of the easy-to-source alternatives suggested in the variations.

Bok Choy (also known as pak choi)

With bok choy, you get two vegetables in one, the crunchy stalks and the earthy green leaves. The stalks are sweet and juicy, and the leaves taste grassy, with a faint cabbagelike flavor.

SELECTION Asian markets carry a dizzying number of bok choy varieties, but supermarkets likely stock only one of the three types listed here.

Choose bok choy with firm, unblemished stalks and vibrant leaves; avoid yel-lowed leaves or stalks with brown wet spots or cracks. Smaller heads gener-ally have more tender greens, which is important if you will be serving them raw. Large heads can have fibrous or sinewy stalks.

PREP Store bok choy in a loosely sealed plastic bag, along with a paper towel to absorb extra moisture, and refrigerate for no more than 2 to 3 days. Unless you plan to halve heads of baby bok choy lengthwise and cook them whole, trim off the bottom inch or so of the stalk and discard. Separate the stalks from the leaves—the stalks take slightly longer to cook—and rinse both parts well in cool water. Slice the bok choy as directed in individual

Bok choy: A single large head weighing 1 to 2 pounds and measuring 12 inches long or more, with white stalks and dark green leaves.

Baby bok choy: Individual heads 4 to 5 inches long, each weighing a few ounces.

Shanghai bok choy: Small heads averaging 6 inches long and weighing about 4 ounces each. Stalks are pale green topped by darker green leaves.

recipes. Bok choy tastes best stir-fried, sautéed, or quick-braised in a flavor-ful liquid. Cook the stalks only briefly, as they get watery if overcooked. The leaves need only a flash in the pan; you can toss them in near the end of cooking. Try the smaller heads of bok choy raw or grilled, too.

NUTRITION Bok choy is high in vitamins C and A and is a good source of fiber, iron, potassium, and B complex vitamins. It has about 9 calories per cup.

Chinese Broccoli (also known as gai lan and Chinese kale)

With its edible stems and dark leaves, Chinese broccoli vaguely resembles broccoli rabe in appearance, but its sweet and juicy flavor is closer to that of broccolini.

SELECTION Chinese broccoli is sold in bunches weighing about 12 ounces each. Choose a bunch with crisp round stems and lots of fresh-looking leaves. Pass up any bunches that show signs of wilting or yellowing. Choose thinner stalks, as the fatter ones are sometimes quite fibrous.

PREP Remove rubber bands or twist ties from bunches and slip the greens, along with a paper towel to wick away excess moisture, into a loosely sealed plastic bag. Refrigerate for no more than 3 to 5 days. When ready to use, trim off about 1/2 inch from the end of each stalk and discard, then rinse the stalks and leaves well. Stir-fry Chinese broccoli, simmer it in soups, or treat it to a quick steam. Stalks take longer to cook than leaves; separate the two parts and add the leaves toward the end of cooking.

NUTRITION Chinese broccoli is high in vitamins C and A, calcium, and iron. It has about 19 calories per cup.

Mizuna

Most often used as a salad green, mizuna is a mild mustard green, crisp and tender with just a hint of bitterness.

SELECTION Mizuna can be hard to find; an Asian grocery or a farmers' market is the most likely source. Look for fresh, feathery bunches of mizuna with pale green or white stalks and long, serrated light green leaves. This brassica is highly perishable, so never buy a bunch that shows signs of yellowing or wilting.

PREP Remove rubber bands or twist ties from bunches and put the leaves in a loosely sealed plastic bag, along with a paper towel to absorb extra moisture. Refrigerate for no more than 2 to 3 days. Trim and discard the stem ends and either coarsely chop the remaining stems or remove them completely—your choice. Wash the greens (see page 7) and dry them well in a salad spinner. Coarsely chop the leaves into bite-size pieces. Mizuna is best served raw or gently wilted.

NUTRITION Mizuna is high in vitamins A and C and in folic acid. It has about 15 calories per cup.

Napa Cabbage (also known as Chinese cabbage)

Napa cabbage is oblong, has a mild, sweet taste and juicy, crisp texture, and is slightly more delicate than its round-headed cousins, due in part to its higher water content. Its wide white stalks and ruffled pale green leaves make it seem more like a cross between bok choy and romaine lettuce than a traditional head of cabbage.

SELECTION Choose elongated heads that feel firm and heavy for their size and with no signs of rot. A few dark speckles on the white part of the stalk are acceptable, but avoid any obvious brown wet spots. An average head weighs about 2 pounds. Do not confuse napa cabbage with savoy cabbage, which is round and lacks a noticeable stalk.

PREP Napa cabbage is considerably more perishable than green, red, or savoy cabbage. Store the head in a loosely sealed plastic bag. Tuck in a paper towel to wick away any excess moisture, then refrigerate for no more than 4 to 7 days. Cut off and discard the stem end of the cabbage before slicing it into pieces as directed in individual recipes. If the stalks are especially wide, halve them lengthwise before cutting crosswise. Wash the cabbage leaves as you would leafy greens (see page 7) and dry them well, especially if they are destined for the salad bowl. Serve napa cabbage raw, or stir-fry it quickly, as it continues to release water as it cooks.

NUTRITION Napa cabbage is high in vitamins A and C, folic acid, and cancer-preventing glucosinolates. It is low in calories, with only about 15 calories per cup.

Tatsoi

Tatsoi can be difficult to find, but be sure to pick up some if you see it. It is an altogether intriguing vegetable, sweet and crisp, somewhat comparable in taste to bok choy leaves.

SELECTION Tatsoi has deep green, spoon-shaped leaves that grow in rosettes. Choose fresh-looking leaves with no yellowing or wilting.

PREP Store tatsoi in a loosely sealed plastic bag with a paper towel to absorb excess moisture, and refrigerate for no more than 2 to 3 days. Separate the leaves from the rosette, if they are still attached. Wash the leaves (see page 7) and dry them well. If you are serving tatsoi raw in a salad, trim off any particularly long stems. Tatsoi tastes great cooked as well; stir-fry it, toss it into soups, or wilt it as you would watercress.

NUTRITION Tatsoi is a great source of vitamins C and A and potassium. It contains about 15 calories per cup.

Garlicky Stir-Fried Bok Choy

SERVES 4

3 tablespoons chicken or vegetable broth

1 tablespoon soy sauce or tamari

½ teaspoon cornstarch, or 1 teaspoon potato starch

1½ tablespoons canola or other neutral oil

4 cloves garlic, thinly sliced

1¼ pounds bok choy, ends trimmed and discarded, stalks and leaves cut into 1-inch pieces (halve the stalks lengthwise if more than 1 inch wide); keep stalks and leaves in separate piles

Kosher salt

I PREFER THE SMALL, pale green heads of Shanghai bok choy in stir-fries for their sweet, delicate flavor, but you can use regular bok choy, as well. If the stalks are wide, halve them lengthwise before cutting into smaller pieces. Be sure to mix the sauce ingredients before you start cooking; the stir-fry happens fast—2 to 3 minutes tops—and you won't want to walk away from the pan. Bok choy tastes watery if it overcooks, so cut the heat when it is crisp-tender.

In a small bowl, stir together the broth, soy sauce, and cornstarch. Be sure the cornstarch dissolves. Set aside until ready to use.

Put the oil and garlic in a large (12 inches or wider) frying pan over medium-high heat. When the garlic starts to sizzle, add the bok choy stalks and cook, stirring frequently, for 1 minute. Add the bok choy leaves to the pan. Give the sauce a quick stir, add it to the pan, and cook the bok choy, stirring to coat it with the sauce, for about 2 minutes more. Remove the pan from the heat while the bok choy is still crisp-tender. Taste and add a pinch of salt if needed. Serve immediately.

VARIATIONS Use this recipe for any type of bok choy (see page 114) or for tatsoi.

OLD-SCHOOL WALDORF SALADS call for a heavy-handed mayonnaise-dressed mix of celery, walnuts, and apples. This updated riff uses raw bok choy instead of celery and a lighter dressing of Greek yogurt with just a dab of mayo, plus a punchy secret ingredient: crystallized ginger. (Look for crystallized ginger in the baking aisle, in the bulk bins area, or near the dried fruits in a grocery store or natural foods store.) Take the time to salt the bok choy (see instructions) before making the salad, giving the vegetable a chance to dump its excess water in the sink instead of your salad. I used small heads of light green Shanghai bok choy, which are slightly less fibrous than the full-size heads.

Bok Choy *and* Crystallized Ginger Waldorf Salad

SERVES 4

1 pound Shanghai bok choy (about 4 heads), ends trimmed and discarded, stalks and leaves halved lengthwise, then cut crosswise into ¼-inch-wide pieces

1 teaspoon kosher salt

½ cup plain 2-percent Greek yogurt

2 tablespoons mayonnaise

Grated zest of 1 lemon

1½ teaspoons freshly squeezed lemon juice

1½ teaspoons honey

1 red apple, diced

½ cup red seedless grapes, halved

½ cup chopped toasted walnuts (see page 13)

3 tablespoons chopped crystallized ginger

Put the bok choy stalks and leaves in a colander in the sink. Sprinkle the salt over the top, then rub it into the bok choy with your fingers briefly. Let the bok choy stand for about 10 minutes to shed its excess liquid.

To make the dressing, in a small bowl, stir together the yogurt, mayonnaise, lemon zest, lemon juice, and honey. Cover and refrigerate until ready to use. (The dressing can be made up to 3 days in advance.)

Give the bok choy a gentle squeeze to release excess liquid and then transfer it to a serving bowl. Add the apple, grapes, walnuts, and ginger to the bowl. Just before serving, using a spatula, gently combine the salad with the dressing.

Grilled Baby Bok Choy *with* Miso Butter

SERVES 4

1½ pounds baby bok choy (about 6 heads) or Shanghai bok choy

3 tablespoons unsalted butter, at room temperature

3 tablespoons white or yellow miso paste (see page 13)

2 tablespoons olive oil

1 tablespoon freshly squeezed lemon juice

Pinch of kosher salt

Freshly ground black pepper

BOILING OR STEAMING bok choy often results in a watery, stringy vegetable. But grilling halved heads of bok choy slathered with miso butter leads to pure flavor. Be sure to keep the heat at medium so the paste can caramelize without burning. My first few attempts at grilling bok choy (I used Shanghai bok choy) resulted in charred leaves that were too crisp to enjoy. Now I separate the leaves from the stalks and use them raw in a salad that wilts under the heat of the grilled vegetable. Use white or yellow miso paste in this recipe. If you use a darker miso, know that it will be saltier. Make this side dish when you are already firing up the grill for the main course.

Cut the leaves away from the bok choy stalks. Halve the stalks lengthwise. Rinse the leaves and stalks well, then pat dry to remove any excess water. In a small bowl, mix together the butter and miso with a fork until well combined. Set aside.

Prepare a medium-hot fire in a charcoal or gas grill. Put the bok choy stalks in a large bowl. Using your hands (or a fork), coat the bok choy with the miso butter. Arrange the bok choy, cut side down, on the grill grate. (If you have a grill screen, set it on top of the grate before adding the bok choy, to keep the stalks from falling through the gaps.) Close the lid and grill for about 5 minutes, until golden brown on the underside. Turn the bok choy with tongs, re-cover, and grill for 5 to 6 minutes more, until golden and crisp-tender.

While the stalks are cooking, stack the bok choy leaves and roll them up lengthwise into a cigar shape. Slice the leaves crosswise into thin shreds. Make a bed of the shredded leaves on a serving platter. Drizzle the leaves with the oil and lemon juice, sprinkle with the salt and ¼ teaspoon pepper, and toss to combine.

Put the grilled bok choy on the dressed salad to wilt the leaves; sprinkle additional pepper over the bok choy. Serve immediately.

WHEN YOU BUY Chinese broccoli (sometimes labeled *gai lan*), it is almost like getting two vegetables in one: toothsome stems and leafy greens. The bulk of the vegetable is comprised of edible stems that are generally about the width of a fat thumb, topped by sturdy, dark green leaves. Unlike broccolini, Chinese broccoli should contain few, if any, florets. To give the stems a chance to cook through, Chinese broccoli is often blanched or steamed before adding it to a stir-fry. I think blanching makes the leaves too wet, so I solve the problem by steaming the stems first with just a touch of water, and then adding the leaves to finish the sauté or stir-fry. Chinese broccoli is seldom stocked in regular grocery stores, so you'll need to stop by an Asian market. It is inexpensive and utterly delicious. Or, try the broccolini variation.

Oyster sauce often contains wheat flour, so if you are following a gluten-free diet, look for a wheat-free brand, such as Lee Kum Kee's green label Panda brand or Wok Mei. If you do not eat soy products, you can omit the soy sauce or substitute Asian fish sauce.

Chinese Broccoli *with* Ginger *and* Oyster Sauce

SERVES 4

2 tablespoons canola or other neutral oil

1 tablespoon peeled, minced fresh ginger

1 pound Chinese broccoli, ends trimmed and discarded, stems cut on the diagonal into ½-inch-wide pieces, leaves cut into ½-inch-wide ribbons (keep stems and leaves in separate piles)

2 tablespoons chicken or vegetable broth

2 tablespoons oyster sauce

1 teaspoon soy sauce or tamari

Put the oil and ginger in a large (12 inches or larger), deep frying pan and place over medium-high heat. When the ginger starts to sizzle, add the Chinese broccoli stems to the pan and cook, stirring, for about 1 minute. Add the broth, cover the pan, and turn down the heat to medium-low. Steam the stems for about 3 minutes, until almost tender. Uncover the pan and raise the heat to medium-high.

Add the leaves to the pan and cook, stirring frequently, for about 1 minute, until starting to wilt. Add the oyster sauce and soy sauce and cook for about 1 minute more, until the sauces coat the stems and leaves. Serve hot.

VARIATION Substitute broccolini for the Chinese broccoli. Trim off about 1 inch of the ends and discard. Cut the remainder into ½-inch pieces. Add the stems and florets to the pan at the same time.

Kimchi Pancakes

SERVES 4 AS AN APPETIZER

2 eggs

1 cup white rice flour

¾ cup cold water

Kosher salt

1 cup finely chopped purchased or homemade napa cabbage kimchi (see recipe), squeezed to remove excess liquid

1½ tablespoons canola or other neutral oil (divided), plus more if needed

ENTIRE BOOKS HAVE BEEN WRITTEN about all of the amazing varieties of kimchi, or Korean fermented vegetables. The most common type is made from napa cabbage, which calls for tossing salted cabbage with a seasoning paste of garlic, ginger, chile powder, green onions, and often salted shrimp and then leaving it to ferment. The first time you try kimchi, you'll likely take note of its spicy, sour brininess, but it's a taste you'll soon find additive. Serve it as a pickle, a side dish, or as an ingredient in kimchi fried rice or these Korean-style pancakes, which can be served as an appetizer, snack, or part of a larger meal. Kimchi is widely available in Asian markets, and it's becoming easier to find in supermarkets and natural foods stores, as well. Look for it in the refrigerated section near the sauerkraut. Because some kimchi contains shrimp or other shellfish, check the label carefully if you are a vegan or have a shellfish allergy. It is also sometimes thickened with wheat flour, so check for that, too, if you are avoiding gluten. Or, if you plan ahead, you can easily make it at home (page 125).

Crack the eggs into a medium bowl and whisk them to combine. Add the rice flour, water, and 1 teaspoon salt and whisk to form a thin batter. Fold in the kimchi.

Line a rimmed baking sheet with paper towels and preheat the oven to 200°F. (Or, you can skip this step and serve the pancakes hot from the pan.) In a 10- to 12-inch nonstick frying pan, heat 1½ teaspoons of the oil over medium-high heat. Stir the batter, then, using a 1-cup measure, scoop out about ¾ cup of the kimchi-laced batter and add it to the pan, forming a thin pancake. Cook the pancake for 3 minutes, then flip it with a spatula. Lower the heat to medium and continue cooking for about 3 minutes longer, until the pancake is light brown on both sides and cooked through. Transfer the pancake to the baking sheet, sprinkle the top with a pinch of salt, and place in the oven to keep warm.

Repeat the process, always stirring the batter well just before adding it to the pan and starting the pancake over medium-high heat. If a pancake threatens to stick, add a little more oil to the pan. You should have 3 pancakes total. Cut the pancakes into wedges to serve.

Cabbage Kimchi

In a large bowl, mix the salt with the water. Add the cabbage to the bowl. If the leaves stick out of the water, place a piece of plastic wrap directly on the surface of the water and then top it with a plate to submerge the cabbage. Let the cabbage soak at room temperature for at least 6 hours or up to overnight.

Meanwhile, in a small bowl, stir together the garlic, chile powder, fish sauce, sugar, and ginger. Refrigerate, covered, until ready to use.

Drain the cabbage in a colander and then squeeze it to remove any excess liquid. Rinse out the bowl, dry it, and return the cabbage to the bowl. Add the green onions and radish and stir to combine. Add the spice paste and mix with a large spatula or your hands until well combined.

Transfer the kimchi and any accumulated liquid to a single large jar with a lid, 2 quart jars with lids, or to a plastic container with a locking lid. The lid is important here, as the kimchi has a strong odor. Let the kimchi stand at room temperature for 48 hours (less if your kitchen is much warmer than room temperature) to start the fermentation process. (You should notice liquid accumulating at the bottom of the jar within the first 24 hours.)

After 48 hours, stir the kimchi and then use it to make the pancakes or serve it as a side dish. To store the remainder, re-cover tightly and refrigerate for up 3 to 4 weeks. The longer you store the kimchi, the stronger its flavor becomes.

$^1/_2$ cup kosher salt

12 cups water

1 large head napa cabbage (3 to 3$^1/_2$ pounds), quartered lengthwise, then cut crosswise into 2-inch pieces

8 cloves garlic, minced

$^1/_4$ cup coarsely ground Korean chile powder

3 tablespoons Asian fish sauce

1 tablespoon sugar

1$^1/_2$ teaspoons peeled, minced fresh ginger

2 green onions, white and green parts, thinly sliced

4 ounces daikon radish, peeled and cut into matchstick strips (about 1 cup)

Asian Brassicas

125

Vietnamese Napa Slaw

SERVES 4

1 small head Napa cabbage (about 1¼ pounds), ends trimmed, leaves separated and cut crosswise into ¼-inch-wide strips (about 8 cups loosely packed)

3 green onions, whites and green parts, thinly sliced

1 cup peeled, shredded carrots

2 tablespoons Asian fish sauce

2 tablespoons freshly squeezed lime juice

¼ teaspoon red pepper flakes

½ cup tightly packed fresh mint and/or cilantro leaves

¼ cup chopped unsalted peanuts

DO NOT SKIMP on the fresh herbs in this Vietnamese-inspired salad. The combination of fresh mint and cilantro used here works especially well, but you can choose one or the other. If you want to turn this easy side dish into a main dish salad, just toss in some shredded chicken. (You may need to add a bit more lime juice or fish sauce; taste and see.) Napa cabbage has a softer texture than other types of cabbage, closer, in fact, to romaine lettuce. To prevent wilting, toss it with the dressing just before serving. If you need to make the salad ahead of time, use sturdier savoy or green cabbage instead. For a vegetarian slaw, substitute soy sauce for the fish sauce.

Put the cabbage, green onions, and carrots in a serving bowl. Just before serving, add the fish sauce, lime juice, red pepper flakes, and herbs and toss to combine. Sprinkle the peanuts over the top of the slaw and serve immediately.

UNLIKE GREEN CABBAGE with its thick and sturdy leaves, napa cabbage has delicate leaves that react quickly to heat. Be sure the leaves are fully dried before you cook them, and serve the stir-fry as soon as it's done—it is best hot anyway—because it gets watery as it sits. Flavored with garlic and cumin—plus sesame seeds for crunch—the cabbage pairs well with almost any meat or seafood main course. I particularly like it alongside something spicy with steamed rice on the side. Look for jars of toasted sesame seeds in the Asian foods aisle of your grocery store or at an Asian market, or toast sesame seeds in a small, dry frying pan over medium-low heat for a minute or two.

Sesame Cabbage Stir-Fry

SERVES 4

2 tablespoons olive oil

2 cloves garlic, minced

1 small head Napa cabbage (about 1½ pounds), ends trimmed, leaves separated and halved lengthwise, then cut crosswise into 1-inch pieces

¾ teaspoon ground cumin

Scant ½ teaspoon kosher salt

2 tablespoons toasted sesame seeds

Put the oil and garlic in a large (12 inches or wider) frying pan or a wok over medium-high heat. When the garlic starts to sizzles, add the cabbage, cumin, and salt and stir-fry for 2 to 3 minutes, until the cabbage is just wilted. Stir in the sesame seeds. Serve hot.

VARIATION The stir-fry works well with savoy cabbage. Since its texture is firmer, it may take a minute or two longer to cook; keep it in the pan until it is wilted to your taste.

YOU GET A DOUBLE DOSE of brassicas in this North African–inspired salad that calls for both mizuna and cauliflower. My husband loves mizuna, a mildly peppery salad green, so we tend to eat a ton of it when it shows up at the farmers' market in early spring. If you cannot find it, baby arugula (another brassica) makes an ideal substitute. Don't forget to add the dates; their honeyed sweetness creates a perfect balance of flavors with the cumin-laced cauliflower and greens. Find fresh dates in the produce section or dried chopped dates near the raisins. I like the taste of honey in the dressing, but for a vegan-friendly version, substitute agave nectar.

Mizuna Salad *with* Cumin-Roasted Cauliflower

SERVES 4

1 small head cauliflower, cored and cut into bite-size florets (about 4 cups)

5 tablespoons olive oil (divided)

¾ teaspoon kosher salt (divided)

1¾ teaspoons ground cumin (divided)

1 tablespoon freshly squeezed lemon juice

1 teaspoon honey

¼ teaspoon freshly ground black pepper

1 large bunch mizuna, large stems removed, or 1 (5-ounce) package baby arugula (about 12 cups loosely packed)

4 fresh or dried dates, pitted and finely chopped (about ½ cup)

Preheat the oven to 450°F. Put the cauliflower on a rimmed baking sheet, drizzle with 2 tablespoons of the oil, sprinkle with $^1/_2$ teaspoon of the salt and $1^1/_2$ teaspoons of the cumin, and toss to coat evenly, then spread in a single layer. Roast the cauliflower, stirring once or twice, for about 15 minutes, until golden brown and tender but not mushy. Taste a floret for doneness; larger florets may take slightly longer to cook.

While the cauliflower is roasting, make the dressing: In a small bowl, whisk together the lemon juice, honey, the remaining $^1/_4$ teaspoon salt and $^1/_4$ teaspoon cumin, and the pepper. Whisk in the remaining 3 tablespoons olive oil.

In a serving bowl, combine the roasted cauliflower, mizuna, and dates, drizzle with the dressing, and toss to coat evenly. Taste and add additional salt and pepper if needed. Serve immediately.

Italian-Style Greens Soup *with* Arborio Rice

SERVES 4

2 tablespoons olive oil

1 small yellow onion, chopped

1 celery stalk, chopped

4 cups chicken or vegetable broth

2 cups water

⅓ cup Arborio rice

1 teaspoon kosher salt

12 ounces Chinese broccoli, tough ends trimmed and discarded, stems and leaves cut crosswise into ½-inch-wide pieces (6 cups)

3 tablespoons grated Parmesan cheese, plus more for serving

Freshly ground black pepper

INSPIRATION FOR THIS SOUP comes from a traditional rustic Italian soup made from escarole and rice. Chinese broccoli leaves and stems make an intriguing substitute for the escarole, adding only a hint of bitterness to the soup. Since the soup is so simple and straightforward, this is the ideal place to use a good homemade broth, if you have one on hand.

In a pot, heat the oil over medium-low heat. Add the onion and celery and cook, stirring occasionally, for about 10 minutes, until starting to soften.

Add the broth, water, rice, and salt to the pot and bring the mixture to a boil. Stir in the Chinese broccoli, turn down the heat to medium-low heat, and simmer for 15 to 20 minutes, until the Chinese broccoli stems are tender and the rice is cooked.

Stir in the Parmesan cheese. Ladle the soup into bowls and top with a generous grind of pepper and additional Parmesan.

VARIATIONS Substitute 6 cups coarsely chopped cabbage (green or savoy) or kale for the Chinese broccoli.

FRIEND AND RECIPE DEVELOPER Jennifer Bryman created this spectacular salad as an interesting way to use tatsoi without incorporating Asian flavors. Frankly, tatsoi is hard to find; if you come across it at an Asian market or farmers' market, be sure to snap it right up. It has a mild, grassy flavor somewhat similar to that of bok choy leaves and tastes terrific raw or tossed into soups and stir-fries. Should the ever-elusive tatsoi fail to appear, don't fret. This salad works great with baby arugula or watercress, as well.

To make the dressing, in a small bowl, whisk together the lime zest, lime juice, honey, cumin, and salt. Whisk in the oil.

Just before serving, toss the tatsoi with the dressing in a large serving bowl. Add the blueberries, walnuts, and feta and toss gently to combine. Serve immediately.

VARIATIONS Substitute watercress or baby arugula for the tatsoi. Organic Girl brand packages a SuperGreens! blend of baby chard, tatsoi, spinach, and arugula; you could use that as well.

Tatsoi *and* Blueberry Salad

SERVES 4

Grated zest of 1 lime

2 tablespoons freshly squeezed lime juice

1 tablespoon honey

½ teaspoon ground cumin

¼ teaspoon kosher salt

2 tablespoons olive oil

2 bunches tatsoi, thick stems removed, leaves halved if large (about 12 loosely packed cups)

1 cup fresh blueberries

⅓ cup chopped walnuts, toasted (see page 13)

⅓ cup crumbled feta cheese

rutabaga   *radish*   *kohlrabi*

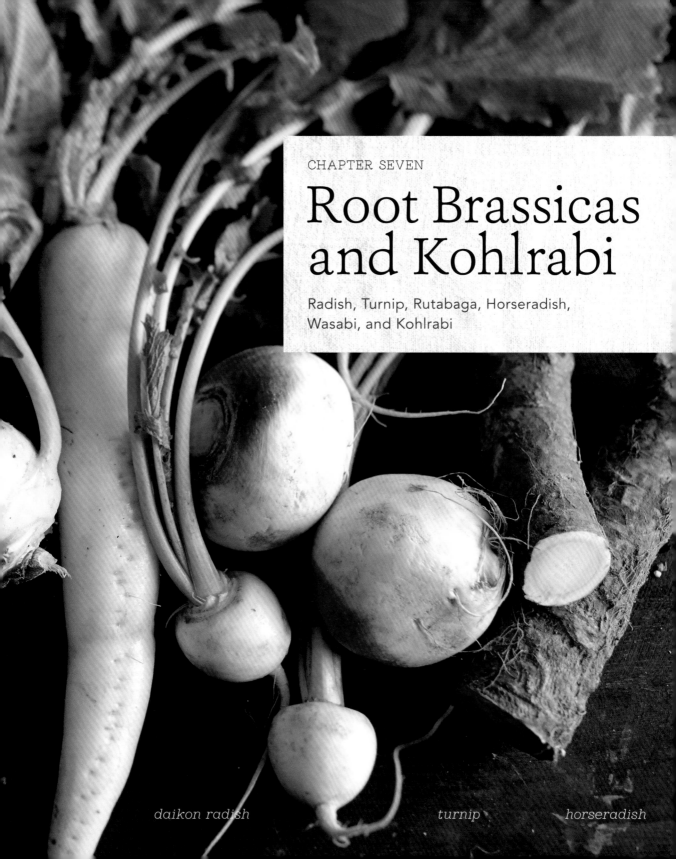

CHAPTER SEVEN

Root Brassicas and Kohlrabi

Radish, Turnip, Rutabaga, Horseradish,
Wasabi, and Kohlrabi

daikon radish   *turnip*   *horseradish*

Unlike the Asian brassicas, which share similar flavor characteristics, the root brassicas are quite diverse, ranging from starchy rutabagas to sinus-clearing horseradish. Wasabi deserves a mention as being part of this illustrious group, but I did not include any recipes because fresh wasabi is so challenging to find and so expensive if you do find it. Although kohlrabi is actually a swollen stem not a root, I have slipped it in here because it fits in this chapter the best.

Radish

There are two basic categories of radishes, table radishes and Asian radishes. The former, most often spotted in salads, are crisp and juicy and have a hot, peppery finish. Cooking sweetens them, muting their bite. Asian radishes such as daikon are crisp and juicy, as well, but have a milder flavor.

SELECTION Table radishes—French breakfast, Icicle, Easter Egg, and Cherry Belle are popular varieties—are sold in bunches. They are typically round or cylindrical and come in several colors, such as white, pink, red, or purple with pure white interiors. Choose firm radishes with no cracks or dry areas, ideally topped with fresh-looking greens. An average bunch contains 8 to 12 radishes.

Daikon radishes are the most common Asian radishes found in supermarkets. These thick cylinders are sold individually, should feel firm, smooth, and heavy for their size, and sometimes weigh up to a few pounds each. Their skin is whitish, sometimes tinted with pale green, and their flesh is ivory.

PREP If you purchase radishes with greens attached, remove the greens and store them separately. Store radishes in a loosely sealed plastic bag, along with a paper towel to wick away excess moisture. Refrigerate table radishes for no more than 5 to 7 days; daikon radishes will keep for up to a few weeks. Wrap the greens in a paper towel and store them in a loosely sealed plastic bag for no more than 2 to 3 days.

When ready to cook, scrub daikon radishes under running water, then peel them. Table radishes are usually quite dirty. I often soak them in a bowl of water for a few minutes—especially the greens—and agitate them in the water to remove any hidden grit. Repeat this process as needed. Trim the stem and the rootlets from radishes before serving. Keep in mind that although table radishes are usually seen raw, they are also delicious roasted or braised. Cooking sweetens them and mellows their sharp bite. Daikon radishes can be served raw or simmered in soups and stews.

NUTRITION Radishes are good sources of vitamins C, A, and B$_6$, as well as calcium, magnesium, and potassium. They have about 20 calories per cup.

Turnip

If you fear turnips as harsh and aggressive, try a bunch of Tokyo turnips in the spring. Sometimes called baby turnips or Japanese turnips, these small, round, white turnips (they have white interiors, too) have a delightful mild, grassy flavor and sweet, juicy texture that will instantly change your mind. Try them sautéed or even raw. Purple-topped storage turnips have a more pronounced flavor that builds as you eat them, but their distinctive pepperiness works well in warming winter stews and braises.

SELECTION Look for bunches of Tokyo turnips topped with fresh green leaves. The turnips should have smooth skin with no cracks or soft spots; avoid wilted or yellowed leaves. The size of a bunch varies but averages 9 to 12 ounces. Tokyo turnips can be hard to find; look for them in Asian markets or farmers' markets. Purple-topped turnips are sold individually and average around 6 ounces each. These turnips are white with light purple tops and white interiors. They should feel heavy for their size and be smooth and crack-free.

PREP If you purchase small turnips with greens attached, remove the greens, discarding the connective stems, and store them separately. Refrigerate turnips in a loosely sealed plastic bag with a paper towel to absorb excess moisture. Tokyo turnips will keep for no more than 3 to 5 days, and purple-topped turnips will keep for up to a few weeks. Wrap the greens in a paper towel and store them in a plastic bag for a day or two. Small young turnips do not need to be peeled but rinse them well before using. Scrub large turnips under running water and peel them before cooking. Wash the greens well (see page 7) and spin them dry.

NUTRITION Turnips are good sources of vitamin C; the greens are more nutritious than the roots, containing vitamins A and K, folate, and calcium, as well. Turnips have about 35 calories per cup; their greens contain about 17 calories per cup.

Rutabaga (also known as swede)

I am not sure why people think poorly of rutabagas. For the most part, they taste "rooty," with a mild sweetness that isn't particularly pungent or aggressive. Some can taste slightly bitter, though still tamer than turnips. Their flesh is starchy and dry, making them almost potato-like in effect. Try them roasted, simmered, or braised.

SELECTION Rutabagas are cream colored with purple tops (as opposed to the white-and-purple combination of turnips) and a creamy pale interior. They are often coated in wax for storage purposes, though try to choose small (7 or 8 ounces each), unwaxed rutabagas whenever possible. Rutabagas are sold individually and almost never have leaves attached. Choose smaller specimens that feel firm and heavy for their size and are free of cracks or soft spots.

PREP Store rutabagas in a loosely sealed plastic bag with a paper towel to wick away extra moisture. They will keep in the refrigerator for 2 to 4 weeks. Scrub rutabagas under running water and peel them before cooking.

NUTRITION Rutabagas are high in potassium, calcium, magnesium, fiber, and vitamins A and C. They contain about 50 calories per cup.

Horseradish

Eating horseradish can provoke one of those pleasure-in-pain moments, vapors sweeping through your sinus cavity with apt precision. Yes, horseradish is pungent and sharp, possibly even tear provoking, but it is also fun to eat.

SELECTION Choose very firm to hard horseradish roots; limp specimens will be spongy inside. Horseradish is light brown, likely covered with dirt, with creamy white flesh inside. Avoid horseradish roots that are green or moldy.

PREP Wrap horseradish root in a damp paper towel and store it in a sealed plastic bag in the refrigerator for up to a few weeks. When you are ready to use it, scrub the root, trim the ends, and peel only as much as you will need. Grate the horseradish on the small holes of a box grater or in a food processor. Watch your eyes, however. Horseradish develops its pungency when grated and will throw off some serious fumes. Wear protective goggles if you are particularly sensitive (seriously), or back away as you remove the lid from the food processor. Toss the grated horseradish with a touch of lemon juice or vinegar to prevent browning. Use horseradish raw or add it toward the end of cooking, since heat somewhat diminishes its pungency.

NUTRITION It would be hard to consume enough horseradish to matter nutritionally, but it does contain vitamin C, potassium, and antibacterial properties.

Wasabi

Not only pungent but also sweet and fragrant, wasabi is most often seen as an accompaniment to sushi. The roots are very expensive and hard to find; check online sources or Asian markets. Freshly grated wasabi is a real treat; be aware that most "wasabi" you are served is actually powdered horseradish or mustard that has been colored with green food coloring. Seek out restaurants that serve the real deal.

Kohlrabi

Such a charming little vegetable, kohlrabi tastes mild and sweet, somewhat reminiscent of broccoli stalks with a faint peppery, turniplike finish. The leaves taste similar to collard greens. Kohlrabi is very juicy and crisp and is at its finest when served raw, though it also braises well.

SELECTION Kohlrabi is sold either as a single bulb or in bunches, with or without leaves attached. The bulb will be either light green or purple, connected to its dark green leaves by a series of thin stems. The interior flesh is white. Choose small kohlrabies—about the size of a baseball—that are smooth and free of cracks. Leaves should be thick and vibrant, not yellowed or wilted.

PREP Separate the leaves from the kohlrabi bulb, discarding the connective stems. Store the bulbs in a loosely sealed plastic bag along with a paper towel to wick away extra moisture. Refrigerate them for no more than 5 to 7 days. Wrap the greens in a paper towel and store them in a loosely sealed plastic bag for a day or two. Use a knife to peel the kohlrabi deeply, removing any fibrous flesh. When cooking the leaves, remove the center rib if particularly thick.

NUTRITION Kohlrabi is high in vitamin C, potassium, fiber, and B vitamins. It has about 36 calories per cup.

Rooty Mash

SERVES 4

1½ pounds rutabagas, peeled and cut into 1-inch cubes

1 pound sweet potatoes, peeled and cut into 1½-inch cubes

3 tablespoons olive oil (divided)

1 teaspoon kosher salt

2 teaspoons chopped fresh thyme

¼ teaspoon freshly ground black pepper

A MASH OF MIXED root vegetables feels like autumn and, in fact, would be the perfect accompaniment to a cool-weather dish of braised short ribs or brisket. I combined rutabagas with sweet potatoes for a vibrant orange color, but you could also add carrots, turnips, celery root, parsnips, or even regular potatoes. Just keep the total weight of the vegetables at 2½ pounds. Rutabagas have a relatively thick skin; if your vegetable peeler is not up to the job, use a paring knife or a chef's knife.

Preheat the oven to 400°F. Put the rutabagas and sweet potatoes on a rimmed baking sheet, drizzle with 2 tablespoons of the oil, sprinkle with the salt and thyme, and toss to coat evenly, then spread in a single layer.

Roast the vegetables, stirring occasionally, for 30 to 40 minutes, until golden brown and tender.

Transfer the vegetables to a bowl and add the remaining 1 tablespoon oil. Mash with a potato masher (or a fork or your masher of choice) until you have a rough, rustic puree. Stir in the pepper. Taste and add additional salt or pepper if needed. Serve hot.

VARIATION Skip the mashing step. Transfer the roasted vegetable cubes to a serving bowl, stir in the pepper, taste and adjust the seasoning, and serve.

MOST PEOPLE CHOP OFF and discard the radish greens without thinking twice, but I like to use every edible part of a vegetable whenever possible. Here, the peppery radish tops act as salad greens, slightly wilted from the heat of the pan. The radishes themselves need only a few moments in a hot oven to mellow their bite and introduce you to a whole new way of enjoying these garden staples. Two bunches of radishes should be enough for four small portions (most bunches contain 8 to 12 radishes), though die-hard radish fans may want more. Be sure to wash the radish greens well to remove the grit.

Preheat the oven to 400°F. Cut the greens off the radishes and set aside. Trim the rootlets and stems from the radishes and discard. Quarter the radishes and coarsely chop the radish greens. Set them aside in separate piles.

Put the quartered radishes on a rimmed baking sheet, drizzle with the oil, sprinkle with the salt, and toss to coat evenly, then spread in a single layer. Roast the radishes for 7 to 8 minutes, until crisp-tender. The flesh of the radishes will change from white to a more translucent appearance.

Remove the pan from the oven, put the radish greens on the hot baking sheet, and toss them with the cooked radishes; the greens should wilt. Add the lemon juice and toss once more.

Transfer the radishes and greens to a serving plate and top with the blue cheese and a generous grind of pepper. Serve hot or at room temperature.

Roasted Radish Salad *with* Blue Cheese

SERVES 4

2 bunches table radishes (such as Icicle, French breakfast, or a red globe variety) with greens

2 tablespoons olive oil

½ teaspoon kosher salt

2 teaspoons freshly squeezed lemon juice

¼ cup crumbled blue cheese

Freshly ground black pepper, for serving

Tropical Radish Rice Salad

SERVES 4

1 cup black rice or brown basmati rice

1 teaspoon kosher salt (divided)

Scant 2 cups water

4 green onions, white and green parts, thinly sliced

1 mango, peeled, pitted, and cut into ½-inch cubes

1 avocado, halved, pitted, peeled, and cut into ½-inch cubes

1 bunch table radishes (such as Icicle, French breakfast, or a red globe variety), trimmed and diced

Grated zest of 1 lime

2½ tablespoons freshly squeezed lime juice

¼ cup olive oil

½ teaspoon freshly ground black pepper

¾ cup chopped fresh cilantro

THIS SUNNY SALAD makes an ideal partner for grilled chicken, shrimp, salmon, or pork. It is perfect for a potluck or even a simple lunch. You can switch around some of the ingredients without sacrificing its tropical feel: try pineapple instead of mango, mint instead of cilantro, or add some fresh chiles. I use black rice, also known as forbidden rice, which looks stunning alongside the vibrant radishes and mango, but a chewy brown basmati tastes just as good. Actually, any variety of rice will work; follow package directions for cooking times and water quantities.

Put the rice in a saucepan with ¼ teaspoon of the salt and the water. Bring to a boil over high heat, turn down the heat to low, cover, and cook for about 45 minutes, or according to package directions, until the rice is tender (if you opt to use white rice, it will cook in less than half the time). Remove the pan from the heat and let the rice steam, covered, for 5 minutes longer. You should have about 3 cups rice. Spread the rice on a baking sheet (to prevent clumping) and let cool to room temperature. (The rice can be made up to 2 days ahead. Cover and refrigerate. Bring to room temperature before finishing the recipe.)

Put the cooled rice in a large bowl. Add the green onions, mango, avocado, and radishes. Scatter the lime zest, lime juice, oil, the remaining ¾ teaspoon salt, the pepper, and cilantro over the top. Using a spatula, gently fold the ingredients together to combine. Taste and add more salt, pepper, or lime juice if needed. Serve at room temperature.

VARIATIONS Diced pineapple or papaya can be used in place of the mango; use about 1¼ cups. If you are a radish fan and want to showcase this brassica, use 2 bunches instead of 1 bunch. Taste and add more lime juice or olive oil if needed.

IF YOU COME ACROSS bunches of tiny white turnips with their greens still attached, buy them. They have a lovely flavor, sweeter and more delicate than their bigger purple-topped cousins and with skin so thin that it doesn't need peeling. Look for turnips labeled "Tokyo" or "Japanese" turnips. You can likely find them throughout the year at Asian markets. Since the greens are not only edible but also delicious, I throw them right into the sauté pan with the turnips. Diced smoked ham pairs well with the faintly bitter vegetable. Ask the clerk at the deli counter to cut a $1/4$- to $1/2$-inch-thick slice of Black Forest ham for you.

Sautéed Spring Turnips *with* Their Greens

SERVES 4

1½ pounds small white turnips with greens attached (2 or 3 bunches)

2 tablespoons olive oil

4 ounces Black Forest or other similar smoked ham, diced

½ teaspoon kosher salt

2 teaspoons cider vinegar

¼ teaspoon freshly ground black pepper

Separate the greens from the turnips, discarding the thin connective stems. Trim the root end from each turnip and discard. Wash the turnips and the greens well and dry them. Halve the turnips and slice them $1/4$ inch thick. Coarsely chop the greens and keep them in a separate pile. You should have about 2 cups turnips and 4 cups greens.

In a large (12 inches or wider) frying pan, heat the oil over medium-high heat. Add the sliced turnips and ham and cook, stirring frequently, for about 3 minutes, until the turnips start to soften. Stir in the salt and turnip greens and cook for about 2 minutes, until the greens wilt. Stir in the vinegar and pepper. Taste and add more salt, pepper, or vinegar if needed. Serve hot or at room temperature.

VARIATIONS If you cannot find turnips with greens, either skip the greens and add a few more sliced turnips or skip the turnips altogether and try the sauté with kale, collards, or mustard greens instead. Cut the greens into narrow ribbons and add them to the pan once the ham starts to sizzle.

SERVE THIS WINTRY BRAISE over rice or couscous (if you are eating a gluten-free diet, look for "couscous" made from corn or rice) or alongside a simple main dish, like roasted chicken thighs. I used common purple-topped turnips here, but if you come across bunches of Tokyo turnips, they would be delicious, as well. If they are tiny and fresh, you don't even need to peel them; just scrub and quarter them. If you like a saucy braise, serve the dish as soon as it is ready. The turnips will absorb the liquid as the dish cools.

Moroccan Turnip *and* Chickpea Braise

SERVES 4

In a large, deep saucepan, heat the oil over medium heat. Add the onion and carrots and cook, stirring occasionally, for 5 minutes. Add the tomato paste, turnips, salt, cumin, and cayenne pepper and stir well. Add the chickpeas and broth, raise the heat to medium-high, and bring to a boil. Turn down the heat to low, cover, and simmer for 15 to 20 minutes, until the vegetables are tender. Stir in the pepper and cilantro. Serve hot.

VARIATION Substitute an equal weight of rutabagas for the turnips. Peel them and cut into 1/2-inch cubes.

2 tablespoons olive oil

1 small yellow onion, thinly sliced

2 carrots, peeled, halved lengthwise, and cut crosswise into ½-inch-thick half-moons

2 tablespoons tomato paste

1 pound turnips, peeled and cut into ¾-inch cubes

1 teaspoon kosher salt

½ teaspoon ground cumin

¼ teaspoon cayenne pepper

1 (14 to 15-ounce) can chickpeas, drained and rinsed

1 cup chicken or vegetable broth

½ teaspoon freshly ground black pepper

⅓ cup chopped fresh cilantro

Turnip *and* Apple Salsa

MAKES ABOUT 4 CUPS

1 pound turnips, trimmed and peeled

½ teaspoon kosher salt

1 Granny Smith apple, finely diced

¼ cup freshly squeezed lime juice

¼ cup chopped fresh cilantro

I USED COMMON purple-topped turnips for this unusual salsa with great success, but I suspect that young Tokyo turnips would taste sweeter and maybe even better. (If you find tiny, very fresh turnips, you can skip peeling them; just scrub them and trim the ends. Grate them in a food processor, rather than on a box grater, to save your knuckles.) The grated turnips need to be salted for a few minutes so they shed their excess liquid. Don't skip this step or the salsa will be watery. Use this time to dice the apple and chop cilantro. Serve the salsa as a snack with tortilla chips, tuck it inside grilled chicken or fish tacos, or spoon it over slices of pork tenderloin. This salsa tastes sweet and bright, which makes it a good counterpoint to spicy foods. But if you want a spicy salsa, add a few jalapeño chile slices to it.

Grate the turnips on the large holes of a box grater or with a food processor fitted with the shredding attachment. Put the grated turnips in a colander in the sink, sprinkle with the salt, and toss to coat evenly. Let the turnips stand for 10 to 15 minutes to release some of their liquid. Squeeze the turnips with your hand to remove most of the liquid—they do not need to be bone-dry—and then transfer them to a serving bowl.

Add the apple, lime juice, and cilantro to the turnips and toss to combine. Taste and add more lime juice or salt if needed. Serve immediately or refrigerate until ready to use. The salsa still tastes great after a day, though it will lose some of its crisp bite.

VARIATION I like the monochromatic look of this salsa, but if you want to add a splash of color, use a tart red apple, such as Honey Crisp or Cameo.

A JAPANESE SOUP such as this one would traditionally be made with dashi, a broth made from *kombu* (seaweed) and dried bonito (a type of fish) flakes, but I wanted to make it accessible for home cooks. (That said, you can certainly make your own dashi and use it here.) You can use any type of miso you like for the soup; choose a white or yellow miso for a sweeter, more delicate soup or a darker red miso for a richer, saltier version. You could even combine more than one type. Add the miso to the soup just before serving; boiling it destroys many of its healthful enzymes.

Put the oil and ginger in a soup pot and place over medium heat. When the ginger starts to sizzle, add the white parts of the green onions, carrot, potato, and salt and cook, stirring occasionally, for about 5 minutes, until the vegetables start to soften. Add the radish and broth and bring to a boil. Lower the heat to a simmer and cook for about 15 minutes, until the vegetables are tender.

Remove the ginger slices from the soup and discard. Put the miso paste in a small heatproof bowl. Ladle about $1/2$ cup of the hot broth from the soup into the miso and stir with a fork until the miso dissolves, then pour it into the soup. Taste the soup and if it is not too salty, add the soy sauce. Stir in the green parts of the green onion. Ladle into bowls and serve hot.

VARIATIONS Substitute sweet potato for the Yukon gold potato. For a heartier soup, add cubes of tofu and heat through just before you stir in the miso. For a peppery finish, stir in a handful of cress just before serving.

Miso Vegetable Soup

SERVES 4

2 tablespoons canola or other neutral oil

2 slices unpeeled fresh ginger, each $1/8$ inch thick

1 bunch green onions, whites and green parts, cut into 1-inch lengths (keep white and green parts in separate piles)

1 large carrot, peeled, halved lengthwise, and cut crosswise into ¼-inch-thick half-moons

1 Yukon gold potato, peeled and cut into ½-inch cubes

½ teaspoon kosher salt

12 ounces daikon radish, peeled, quartered lengthwise, and cut crosswise into ¼-inch-thick slices (about 2 cups)

4 cups chicken or vegetable broth

¼ cup miso paste, any color (see page 13)

1 tablespoon soy sauce or tamari, if needed

Roasted Rutabagas *with* **Rosemary** *and* **Maple**

SERVES 4

2 pounds rutabagas, peeled and cut into 1-inch cubes

2 tablespoons olive oil

2 teaspoons pure maple syrup

1 tablespoon minced fresh rosemary

¾ teaspoon kosher salt

I CONSTANTLY STRIVE to introduce new vegetables at the family dinner table, and the great rutabaga experiment worked like a charm. The diced rutabagas not only look just like roasted potatoes but have that same starchy quality, as well. The flavor is more pronounced—a kind of "autumnal rootiness"—but it is neither sharp nor bitter. Toss the cubes with the seasonings just before you pop them in the oven. One time I left the seasoned cubes on the counter for about an hour and the salt drew an entire puddle of water out them. The addition of maple syrup adds a sweetness to this dish that makes it a good accompaniment to roast pork, grilled sausages, or a sautéed ham steak.

Preheat the oven to 400°F. Put the rutabagas on a baking sheet, drizzle with the oil and maple syrup, sprinkle with the rosemary and salt, and toss to coat evenly, then spread in a single layer.

Roast the rutabagas, stirring once or twice, for 35 to 40 minutes, until golden brown and tender. Taste and add additional salt if needed. Serve hot or at room temperature.

VARIATIONS Omit the maple syrup and rosemary and add 1¹/₂ teaspoons sweet paprika with the salt. Or, for a nice finishing touch, drizzle a few teaspoons of walnut oil over the rutabagas the moment they come out of the oven.

HORSERADISH SAUCE TRADITIONALLY gets its richness from sour cream or heavy cream, but this healthier version made with plain yogurt tastes just as great. Be sure to purchase Greek yogurt, which is thicker and less watery than regular yogurt. To grate the horseradish, peel the root and run it over the small holes of a box grater. Or, if the sinus-clearing vapors are too potent, cut the peeled horseradish into chunks and process them in a food processor for about a minute, until minced (see pages 136–137 for ideas on how to survive the potent fumes). The recipe calls for a generous amount of grated horseradish, which consequently produces a boldly flavored sauce. If you think it may be too bold, start out with a smaller amount (maybe 1/4 cup) and adjust as needed.

Serve the sauce as an accompaniment to roast beef or pork, poached salmon, or grilled steak. It can also be used as a topping for baked potatoes, as a dressing for a beet salad (the salad will turn pink!), as a dip for raw vegetables, especially cucumbers, or as a sandwich spread. Dollop a spoonful over hard-boiled eggs, or combine it with the cooked yolks and use as a filling for deviled eggs.

Horseradish-Dill Cream

MAKES ABOUT 1 1/3 CUPS

1 cup plain full-fat Greek yogurt

1/3 cup loosely packed grated fresh horseradish (from a 2 ounce piece about 4 inches long by 1 inch wide)

2 teaspoons freshly squeezed lemon juice

1 1/2 teaspoons olive oil

1/2 teaspoon kosher salt

1/4 teaspoon freshly ground black pepper

3 tablespoons chopped fresh dill

In a small bowl, stir together the yogurt, horseradish, lemon juice, oil, salt, and pepper. Add the dill and stir to combine. Cover and refrigerate the cream for at least an hour or two to develop the flavors. Serve chilled. Store any leftover sauce in an airtight container for up to 2 days.

Mushroom *and* Buckwheat Soup *with* Horseradish Gremolata

SERVES 4 TO 6

½ ounce dried sliced porcini or shiitake mushrooms (about ½ cup)

1 cup warm water

2 tablespoons olive oil (divided)

1 yellow onion, chopped

12 ounces white button mushrooms, coarsely chopped

1 teaspoon kosher salt

1 bay leaf

½ cup buckwheat groats

½ cup dry white wine

4 cups beef or mushroom broth

½ teaspoon freshly ground black pepper

1 (3-ounce piece) fresh horseradish root (about 4 inches long by 1½ inch wide)

2 teaspoons white wine vinegar

½ cup chopped fresh flat-leaf parsley

HERE, HEARTY BUCKWHEAT groats paired with fresh and dried mushrooms deliver a winter soup that is satisfying on its own, yet becomes extra special with the added kick of fresh horseradish. Buckwheat groats are the tiny pyramidal, light green or tan seeds of the buckwheat plant. (You may be familiar with kasha, or toasted buckwheat groats.) They are a lovely chewy addition to this soup, where their texture recalls that of barley. Bob's Red Mill is a widely available brand of buckwheat groats; look for it in natural foods stores or the natural foods aisle of your grocery store. Despite the presence of *wheat* in its name, buckwheat groats are gluten-free.

As soon as you have grated the horseradish, mix it with the vinegar to keep it from browning. I find that horseradish provides the most flavor when it is stirred into the soup just before serving, so I ladle the soup into bowls and pass the horseradish-and-parsley mixture at the table.

Put the dried mushrooms and water in a small bowl. Let the mushrooms soak for at least 10 to 15 minutes while you start the soup.

In a soup pot, heat 1 tablespoon of the oil over medium heat. Add the onion and cook, stirring occasionally, for about 5 minutes, until starting to soften. Add the remaining 1 tablespoon oil and raise the heat to medium-high. Add the fresh mushrooms and salt and cook, stirring occasionally, for about 10 minutes, until the mushrooms start to brown. (The mushrooms will initially release a lot of liquid; once the liquid is reabsorbed, the mushrooms will brown. Be patient.)

While the fresh mushrooms are cooking, remove the dried mushrooms from the bowl, reserving the soaking liquid, and chop them. Pour the soaking liquid into a measuring cup, leaving any grit behind in the bowl. Add enough water to the measuring cup to total 1½ cups.

When the fresh mushrooms have browned, add the dried mushrooms, bay leaf, and groats and stir well. Add the wine, broth, and the 1½ cups liquid, raise the heat to high, and bring the soup to a boil. Turn down the heat to a simmer, cover partially, and cook for 15 to 20 minutes, until the buckwheat is tender. Stir in the pepper.

While the soup simmers, peel and grate the horseradish on the small holes of a box grater or in a food processor—you want about $1/2$ cup—and put it in a small bowl. Stir in the vinegar and parsley.

When the soup is ready, ladle it into bowls. Pass the horseradish mixture at the table, inviting guests to stir about 2 tablespoons (or to taste) into their serving. If you end up with leftovers, refrigerate the extra soup and horse-radish separately, both tightly covered. They will keep for up to 2 days. Keep in mind that the groats will continue to absorb the liquid as the soup cools. If the soup gets too thick, add more broth or water as needed.

Kohlrabi Crudités *with* Creamy Feta Dip

SERVES 4

½ cup packed roasted red bell pepper strips (jarred is fine; pat them dry)

1 small clove garlic, minced

¼ teaspoon dried oregano

8 ounces well-drained feta cheese (about 1½ cups crumbled)

2 tablespoons olive oil

1 tablespoon freshly squeezed lemon juice, plus more for serving

Freshly ground black pepper

3 kohlrabi bulbs (about 1¼ pounds total), peeled, halved, and cut into ⅓-inch-thick slices

I KNOW WHAT YOU ARE THINKING. Why is there a "recipe" for raw kohlrabi? Truth be told, kohlrabi tastes great raw. In fact, I prefer raw kohlrabi over cooked. Crisp and juicy, with a pleasantly mild flavor somewhat like a cross between jicama and broccoli stems, kohlrabi is a surprising improvement over the typical crudité platter of celery and carrots. It is sturdy for dipping, paired here with a tangy Greek-inspired blend of feta cheese, roasted bell peppers, and oregano. (Try the dip with cucumbers or cooked chilled shrimp, too.) Use a paring knife or a chef's knife to cut the peel away from the kohlrabi; a vegetable peeler may not be up to the task. Peel deeply enough to get past the fibrous exterior.

Put the pepper strips and garlic in a food processor and puree until smooth. Add the oregano, feta, oil, and lemon juice and pulse to combine. Leave the dip a bit chunky or puree until completely smooth, as you prefer. (If you have only a blender, puree the peppers with the oil and garlic and mix in the remaining ingredients by hand.) Season the dip with black pepper and with additional lemon juice if needed. You should have 1½ cups dip.

Put the kohlrabi slices on a serving plate, drizzle with a touch of lemon juice, and toss to coat evenly. Grind black pepper over the top. Serve the kohlrabi slices with the dip.

VARIATIONS Substitute lightly steamed broccoli florets or roasted cauliflower florets or Brussels sprouts for the kohlrabi.

KOHLRABI IS ONE OF THOSE VEGETABLES that you might spy at the farmers' market and then pass up for lack of familiarity. If I can convince you to try only one new vegetable, I urge you to experiment with kohlrabi. It is fantastic raw, but I also like pairing it with Indian spices and coconut milk for a tasty vegetable curry. Look for kohlrabi that still has its leaves attached; the thick, sturdy greens remind me of collards and make a welcome addition to the curry. Serve this with rice as a side dish to something very simple—maybe grilled chicken—or with steamed quinoa as a vegetarian main course.

Cut the leaves away from the kohlrabi bulbs, discarding the connective stems. (If they lack greens, using just the bulbs is fine.) Wash the greens, dry them, and chop coarsely. Using a paring knife or a chef's knife, peel the bulbs. You must peel deeply enough to remove any fibrous parts; the inside should be crisp and moist. Quarter the bulbs through the stem end and then cut each quarter into 1/4-inch-thick slices. Reserve the kohlrabi slices and leaves in separate piles.

Put the oil and ginger in a large (12 inches or wider), deep frying pan and place over medium heat. When the ginger starts to sizzle, add the onion and bell pepper and cook, stirring occasionally, for about 5 minutes, or until they start to soften. Add the chile, kohlrabi slices, cumin, salt, coriander, and turmeric and stir to coat the vegetables with the spices.

Add the coconut milk and broth to the pan, raise the heat to medium-high, and bring to a simmer. Turn down the heat to low, cover partially, and cook, stirring occasionally, for about 10 minutes, until the vegetables are almost tender. Stir the kohlrabi leaves into the curry and simmer for 5 minutes, until the vegetables are tender. Remove the ginger slices from the curry and discard. Taste and add additional salt if needed. Serve hot. Pass the cilantro, lime wedges, and additional chile slices at the table.

VARIATIONS If you cannot find kohlrabi, substitute 1 pound broccoli, including both the florets and peeled sliced stalks. Or, use 1 bunch collard greens. Remove the center rib and stems and coarsely chop the leaves. Add the broccoli or collard greens along with the spices.

Kohlrabi Curry

SERVES 4

3 kohlrabi bulbs, with leaves if possible (about 1 1/2 pounds total with stems and leaves)

2 tablespoons canola or other neutral oil

2 slices unpeeled fresh ginger, each 1/4 inch thick

1 yellow onion, diced

1 red bell pepper, cut into 1-inch pieces

1 jalapeño chile, seeded and thinly sliced, plus more chile slices, for serving

1 1/2 teaspoons ground cumin

1 1/2 teaspoons kosher salt

1 teaspoon ground coriander

1/2 teaspoon ground turmeric

1 (14 to 15-ounce) can coconut milk

1/2 cup chicken or vegetable broth

Chopped fresh cilantro and lime wedges, for serving (optional)

Root Brassicas and Kohlrabi

Brassicas and Your Health: Special Issues

BY DR. SAMANTHA BRODY

BRASSICAS AND THYROID HEALTH

It is a common directive given by nutritionists, naturopathic physicians, and other alternative health care practitioners that one should not eat raw brassicas because they can suppress thyroid function due to their goitrogenic properties. A *goitrogen* is a compound that causes the thyroid gland to enlarge, or form a goiter, a condition associated with low thyroid function (hypothyroidism). Among the most common symptoms are fatigue, depression, slow metabolism, constipation, and cold hands and feet.

For years I, too, counseled patients to avoid raw brassicas. But then I decided to dig into the research a little more. While it is theoretically true that these compounds present in brassicas can cause a goiter to develop, there are only a few known situations outside of animal studies where it has actually occurred. For example, an article in the May 20, 2010 issue of the *New England Journal of Medicine* documented the case[1] of an eighty-eight-year-old woman who had been eating two to three *pounds* of bok choy daily for several months believing that it would treat her diabetes. Instead, it threw her into a thyroid crisis that put her in the hospital in a coma.

Here's the deal: Those same glucosinolates that have anticancer properties when broken down by certain enzymes become a class of chemicals called thiocyanates. Thiocyanates may decrease the uptake of iodine in the thyroid gland itself, and iodine is an important part of making active thyroid hormone. That said, in order for the enzyme to do this, the brassica *must* be raw (when the vegetables are cooked the enzyme is deactivated) and *must* be crushed (for example, by chewing or cutting).

So again, although it is theoretically possible to cause or increase a hypothyroid state with raw brassicas, the chances of this actually occurring are slim. Could you make it happen? Possibly. Some combination of existing thyroid disease and/or iodine deficiency and consuming large amounts of raw brassicas would be the way to do it. I do have one patient with an existing thyroid condition who was eating a full bunch of raw kale every day for lunch for three to four months. Although this seemed to have had no impact on her thyroid laboratory tests nor did it produce any symptoms, I did suggest that she swap out the kale for lettuce if she's going to keep up the salads. The take-home? If you want to err on the safe side, do not eat piles of these vegetables raw on a regular basis, especially if you have hypothyroidism. Cooked? No problem, eat to your heart's content.

1. M. Chu, "Myxedema Coma Induced by Ingestion of Raw Bok Choy." *New England Journal of Medicine* 362 (May 20, 2010): 1945–46. dOI: 10.1056/NEJMc0911005.

BRASSICAS, VITAMIN K, AND WARFARIN

Warfarin (also known by the brand names Coumadin and Jantoven) is a medication that is used primarily to prevent stroke due to blood clots. It prevents blood from clotting too much by reducing the liver's ability to use vitamin K to make proteins called "clotting factors." Warfarin is even referred to as a vitamin K antagonist, in that it works *against* the function of vitamin K, thus decreasing blood clotting. But what does this have to do with brassicas?

Some of the brassicas contain high amounts of vitamin K (kale and collards, for instance), and others contain moderately high amounts (cabbage, broccoli, Brussels sprouts, turnip greens, mustard greens, broccoli rabe). If a person is on warfarin and eats a significant amount of these vegetables, it could easily have an interaction with his or her medication, causing it to not work effectively. It is typical for patients to be asked to avoid dark green vegetables and certain brassicas entirely. But given how healthful these foods are, it seems wrong to eliminate them.

There *is* a solution, however. Physicians must carefully adjust warfarin to come up with just the right dose for the patient. It is necessary to have regular follow-up blood tests to make sure that the dose is correct (in recent years, some physicians have been sending patients home with kits to do their own blood tests). The trick is to make sure that the medication is titrated to a stable and steady amount of vitamin K in the patient's diet. So really, a simple list of how much vitamin K is in which foods and for what serving size would allow the patient to eat the same amount of vitamin K every day and the dose of warfarin could be adjusted to that serving size. It is a great way to be sure you get your leafy greens daily!

Remember, if you are on warfarin, before you start eating more brassicas, speak with your physician about how to proceed safely. Or, ask your physician about newer anticoagulant medications that don't interact with vitamin K. Hopefully your physician will work with you so that you can eat plenty of these healthful and delicious vegetables.

DR. SAMANTHA BRODY *is a licensed naturopathic physician and acupuncturist and the owner and founder of Evergreen Natural Health Center in Portland, Oregon. She earned her doctoral degree in naturopathic medicine in 1996 and a master's degree in Oriental medicine in 2001 from the National College of Natural Medicine. For more information, go to DrSamantha.com.*

Special Diets

Many people must observe or have chosen to observe certain dietary restrictions. Here are tips for using the recipes in this book if you are adhering to a gluten-free or soy-free diet. For information on other dietary restrictions, see individual recipes and the Special Diets Table on page 158.

GLUTEN-FREE DIET

All of the recipes here are gluten-free, but soy sauce, various types of purchased broth, miso paste, and Dijon mustard often contain wheat, barley, or rye. Read labels carefully and pass up those that list any of these gluten-containing grains. In the case of soy sauce, you can substitute a gluten-free soy sauce or gluten-free tamari. Gluten-free broths are now being produced by a number of companies, including Pacific and Imagine brands. Most types of miso should only contain soybeans, rice, enzymes, and salt, but be aware that barley miso does exist.

Some people complain of problems with bloating and gas after eating brassicas, specifically cabbage, broccoli, cauliflower, and Brussels sprouts. My first advice is to avoid eating hard-textured brassicas, such as broccoli or cauliflower, raw. Beyond that, there are two primary theories as to what causes this reaction and some possible solutions.

Fiber: One of my culinary-school instructors used to call broccoli "nature's little broomsticks," and with good reason. Many brassicas are high in fiber, in general a positive quality, but if your body isn't used to processing a lot of fiber, you may need to build up your tolerance gradually. Introduce high-fiber foods slowly and give your digestive system a head start by chewing your food thoroughly.

Raffinose: Found in brassicas, grains, and other foods, this hard-to-digest sugar travels all the way to your colon before it is "digested" by bacteria. Depending on the fortitude of your intestinal flora, this process can run smoothly or not. If you have trouble digesting brassicas, consider taking a probiotic supplement or regularly including probiotic-rich foods, such as yogurt or kefir, in your diet.

SOY-FREE DIET

Soy sauce and miso paste are the only soy-based ingredients used in these recipes. Asian fish sauce and coconut aminos (made by mixing aged coconut sap with sea salt) are good substitutes for soy sauce. Both Miso Master and South River Miso brands make a chickpea miso paste that can be used in place of the traditional soy-based paste.

SPECIAL DIETS TABLE

The prevalence of food allergies and sensitivities has skyrocketed in recent years. Whether your reasons for following a special diet are medical or simply a personal choice, I want to offer you every opportunity to enjoy as many *Brassicas* recipes as possible. The information you need to make an informed decision is all right here, enabling you to recognize at-a-glance which recipes best suit your needs.

The purpose of this table is twofold. First, I identify which recipes are vegetarian or vegan by labeling them with an "X" in the corresponding column. If a recipe is not vegetarian or vegan, but there is an option within the recipe making it so, the column is marked with an "O" for option. A full 90 percent of the recipes can be made either vegetarian or vegan. Note that sometimes the only ingredient preventing a recipe from being vegetarian is chicken broth, which can be easily substituted.

The remaining columns identify major food allergens, including fish, shellfish, dairy, eggs, soy, peanuts, tree nuts, coconut and sesame. All of the recipes are gluten-free. (Only one recipe—Garlicky Stir-Fried Bok Choy—contains corn, but it also includes an alternative.) These columns are marked with an "X" if the recipe contains that ingredient, or an "O" if it contains the ingredient but there is an option to substitute or exclude it.

Special Diets Table

X = VEGETARIAN OR VEGAN OR CONTAINS LISTED INGREDIENT

O = VEGETARIAN OR VEGAN OPTION OR INGREDIENT SUBSTITUTION AVAILABLE

RECIPE TITLE	Vegetarian	Vegan	Meat	Fish (F) or shellfish (S)	Dairy	Eggs	Soy (see page 157)	Peanuts (P) or tree nuts (T)	Coconut	Sesame
Bok Choy and Crystallized Ginger Waldorf Salad, page 119	X				X			T		
Boke Bowl Cauliflower and Brussels Sprout Salad with Thai Vinaigrette, page 43				F						
Braised Sauerkraut with Apples and Cider, page 66		X								
Brassica Sprouts Salad with Avocado-Lime Cream, page 88		X								
Broccoli and Pepper Jack Frittata, page 82	X				X	X				
Broccoli Rabe with Romesco Sauce, page 104		X						T		
Brussels Sprout Leaves with Lemony Yogurt Dressing, page 57	X				X			T (O)		
Cabbage Confetti Quinoa, page 70	X	O			O					
Caldo Verde, page 32			X							
Cauliflower Hummus, page 47		X								X
Cauliflower Rice, page 51		X								
Cauliflower Soup with Gingerbread Spices, page 46	O	O			O					
Cauliflower with Salsa Verde, page 41		X								
Charred Brussels Sprouts with Pancetta and Fig Glaze, page 58			X							
Chinese Broccoli with Ginger and Oyster Sauce, page 123				S			O			
Citrusy Green Smoothie, page 20		X							O	
Classic Sautéed Broccoli Rabe with Garlic and Anchovies, page 105				F						
Clyde Common's Broccoli Rabe Salad with Pistachios and Lemon Vinaigrette, page 102	O		O			X		T		
Colcannon with Brussels Sprout Leaves, page 62	O	O			O					
Creamy Cauliflower Gratin, page 44	O				X			T		
Creamy Leek and Broccoli Soup, page 84		O								
Curried Collard Greens, page 98	X	O			O					
Five-Spice Red Cabbage Salad, page 64		X						T		

X = VEGETARIAN OR VEGAN OR CONTAINS LISTED INGREDIENT

O = VEGETARIAN OR VEGAN OPTION OR INGREDIENT SUBSTITUTION AVAILABLE

RECIPE TITLE	Vegetarian	Vegan	Meat	Fish (F) or shellfish (S)	Dairy	Eggs	Soy (see page 157)	Peanuts (P) or tree nuts (T)	Coconut	Sesame
Garlicky Stir-Fried Bok Choy, page 118		O					O			
Greek Shaved Cabbage and Fennel Salad, page 63	X				X					
Grilled Baby Bok Choy with Miso Butter, page 120	X				X		O			
Grilled Broccoli with Mustard Vinaigrette and Blue Cheese, page 80	X				X					
Horseradish- Dill Cream, page 149	X				X					
Indian Potato and Cauliflower Curry page 39		X							O	
Italian-Style Greens Soup with Arborio Rice, page 130	O				X					
Kale and Egg Muffins, page 33	O		O			X				
Kale and Sweet Potato Sauté, page 27		X								
Kale Pesto, page 24		X						T		
Keralan-Style Brussels Sprouts, page 60		X							X	
Kimchi Pancakes, page 124	O			F		X				
Kohlrabi and Broccoli Stalk Slaw, page, 77		X					O			X
Kohlrabi Crudités with Creamy Feta Dip, page 152	X				X					
Kohlrabi Curry, page 153		O							X	
Lemony Broccoli Chop, page 79		X								
Lemony Kale Shreds with Salty Cheese, page 21	X	O			O					
Master Kale Sauté, page 18		X								
Mexican Pickled Vegetables, page 50		X								
Miso Vegetable Soup, page 147		O					O			
Miso-Glazed Kale and Shiitakes, page 29		X					O			
Mizuna Salad with Cumin- Roasted Cauliflower, page 129	X	O								
Moroccan Turnip and Chickpea Braise, page 145		O								
Mushroom and Buckwheat Soup with Horseradish Gremolata, page 150		O								
Mustard Greens with Caramelized Sweet Onion, page 101		X								
Peppery Greens Salad, page 107	X				X					
Quick Collards Sauté, page 96		X								
Red Curry Soup with Broccoli and Shrimp, page 85				F, S					X	
Roasted Broccoli with Savory Granola, page 81		X						T		

continued

| | | | | CONTAINS | | | | | | |
RECIPE TITLE	Vegetarian	Vegan	Meat	Fish (F) or shellfish (S)	Dairy	Eggs	Soy (see page 157)	Peanuts (P) or tree nuts (T)	Coconut	Sesame
Roasted Broccolini with Winey Mushrooms, page 87	X	O			O					
Roasted Brussels Sprouts with Parmesan Crust, page 56	X				X					
Roasted Cabbage Wedges with Lemon-Thyme Vinaigrette, page 68		X								
Roasted Cauliflower with Pickled Peppers and Mint, page 42	X	O			O			T (O)		
Roasted Kale Chips, page 25		X								
Roasted Radish Salad with Blue Cheese, page 139	X				X					
Roasted Rutabagas with Rosemary and Maple, page 148		X								
Roman Cauliflower Sauté, page 38	X				X					
Romanesco Summer Salad, page 48		X								
Rooty Mash, page 138		X								
Rustic Vegetable Soup, page 71	O	O			O					
Sausage, Kale, and White Bean Stew, page 30			X		O					
Sautéed Spring Turnips with Their Greens, page 143			X							
Sesame Cabbage Stir-Fry, page 127		X								X
Smoky Kale Salad with Toasted Almonds and Egg, page 22	X	O				O		T		
Spanish Tortilla with Mustard Greens, page 100	X					X				
Spicy Kale Fried Rice, page 28	X	O				O	O			
Spicy Soba Noodles with Wilted Watercress, page 109		X					O			X
Steam-Sautéed Broccoli, page 76		O								
Sunshine Wraps, page 99		X						P		
Tatsoi and Blueberry Salad, page 131	X				X			T		
Tropical Radish Rice Salad, page 140		X								
Turnip and Apple Salsa, page 146		X								
Vietnamese Napa Slaw, page 126	O			F (O)				P		
Watercress Salad with Ginger Carrot Dressing, page 106		X					O			X
White Pizza with Arugula and Prosciutto, page 110	O		X		X					
Wilted Brussels Sprouts with Bacon and Tomatoes, page 61		O	X							

X = VEGETARIAN OR VEGAN OR CONTAINS LISTED INGREDIENT

O = VEGETARIAN OR VEGAN OPTION OR INGREDIENT SUBSTITUTION AVAILABLE

Acknowledgments

Many friends and colleagues shared their knowledge and talents in support of my in-depth look at brassicas. My love and gratitude to each of the following people:

Huge thanks to a special group of friends—my brassica tasting team—for spending countless hours in my kitchen (and theirs) fine-tuning my work: Catarina Hunter, Natasha Pereira, Laura Ford, Shelby Quintos, Sara Conte, Lynne Asgharzadeh, Kyra Bussanich, Susan Terrell, and Barbara Cohen. I miss our brassica lunch extravaganzas! Thanks to Sarah Remy for her magical ways with cabbage and Michelle Janke for additional recipe testing.

Portland, Oregon food writers—and friends—Danielle Centoni, Ivy Manning, Katherine Cole, Diane Morgan, Deena Prichep, Kathleen Bauer, and Martha Holmberg never fail to offer sage advice, toss around recipes, and inspire new ideas. I love the collaborative nature of our community!

Jennifer Bryman, a very talented recipe developer, contributed several fantastic recipes to the book, including one of my favorites, Tatsoi and Blueberry Salad.

PR maven Lisa Hill, whose enthusiastic championing of brassicas may just turn every last broccoli-phobe into a brassica lover!

My intern, Zoe Ching, knows more about food than any twenty-one-year-old I've ever met, and I thank her for her kitchen assistance, last-minute grocery-store runs, and especially for diving headfirst into a massive brassica research project.

Sharon Bowers, my agent, for fueling my fire. It *was* time to write another book. Copy editor Sharon Silva, who tidied up my loose ends with an expert's eye. Photographer Sang An and food stylist George Dolese and their teams for bringing my recipes to life through their stunning photos.

Working with everyone at Ten Speed Press makes me feel like I'm part of a dream team. My gratitude and appreciation go out to publisher Aaron Wehner and my editors Jenny Wapner and Hannah Rahill for guidance and support, Katy Brown for design expertise, and Kara Van de Water for publicity.

Most important, love to my husband, Patrick, and our children, William and Audrey. I thrive on feeding you delicious food every single day and I hope you never tire of eating it.

Contributors

A personal goal of mine is to bring together chefs and food writers with members of the medical community in a united effort to get people back in the kitchen. What better way to take charge of your own health than through cooking? My thanks to the following contributors for sharing their recipes or thoughtful words in pursuit of this common goal:

- Rebecca Katz, MS, chef, author, and educator
- Dr. Samantha Brody, Naturopathic physician and licensed acupuncturist, Evergreen Natural Health Center, Portland, Oregon
- Andrea Nakayama, functional nutritionist, Replenish PDX
- Jennifer Bryman and Mollie Dickson, The Heart's Kitchen
- Patrick Fleming, chef and co-owner, Boke Bowl, Portland, Oregon
- Chris DiMinno, chef, Clyde Common, Portland, Oregon

Selected Bibliography

BOOKS

Bishop, Jack. *Vegetables Every Day*. New York: HarperCollins, 2001.

Kafka, Barbara, with Christopher Styler. *Vegetable Love*. New York: Artisan, 2005.

Kunz, Gray, and Peter Kaminsky. *The Elements of Taste*. Boston: Little, Brown, 2001.

Madison, Deborah. *Local Flavors*. New York: Broadway Books, 2002.

———. *Vegetarian Cooking for Everyone*. New York: Broadway Books, 1997.

McGee, Harold. *On Food and Cooking*. New York: Scribner, 2004.

Morgan, Diane. *Roots*. San Francisco: Chronicle Books, 2012.

Oseland, James. *Cradle of Flavor*. New York: W. W. Norton, 2006.

Ottolenghi, Yotam. *Plenty*. San Francisco: Chronicle Books, 2011.

Peterson, James. *Vegetables*. New York: William Morrow, 1998.

Schneider, Elizabeth. *Uncommon Fruits and Vegetables*. New York: William, 1986.

———. *Vegetables from Amaranth to Zucchini*. New York: HarperCollins, 2001.

Shimbo, Hiroko. *The Japanese Kitchen*. Boston: Harvard Common Press, 2000.

Slater, Nigel. *Tender*. Berkeley, CA: Ten Speed Press, 2009.

Waters, Alice. *Chez Panisse Vegetables*. New York: HarperCollins, 1996.

Wood, Rebecca. *The New Whole Foods Encyclopedia*. New York: Penguin Books, 2010.

Yin-Fei Lo, Eileen. *Mastering the Art of Chinese Cooking*. San Francisco: Chronicle Books, 2009.

WEBSITES

Linus Pauling Institute, www.lpi.oregonstate.edu

USDA Agricultural Research Service, www.ars.usda.gov

USDA Agricultural Library, www.ndb.nal.usda.gov

The World's Healthiest Foods, www.whfoods.org

Index

For William and Audrey

Having children who appreciate good food is a dream come true. I love fielding your requests for homemade waffles on weekdays and even your eleventh-hour calls for braised rabbit or lamb ragù. Now, if you would only eat more brassicas . . .

Published in the United States by Ten Speed Press,
an imprint of the Crown Publishing Group, a division
of Random House LLC, a Penguin Random House
Company, New York.
www.crownpublishing.com
www.tenspeed.com

Ten Speed Press and the Ten Speed Press colophon are
registered trademarks of Random House LLC

Library of Congress Cataloging-in-Publication Data

Russell, Laura B.
  Brassicas: cooking the world's healthiest vegetables:
Kale, Cauliflower, Broccoli, Brussels Sprouts and More /
Laura B. Russell. — First edition.
       pages cm
  Includes bibliographical references and index.
1. Cooking (Vegetables) 2. Brassica. I. Title.
 TX801.R87 2014
 641.6'5—dc23

                              2013031277

Hardcover ISBN: 978-1-60774-571-6
eBook ISBN: 978-1-60774-572-3

Printed in China

Design by Katy Brown
Food Styling by George Dolese

10 9 8 7 6 5 4 3 2 1

First Edition

MAY 0 6 2014